THE FAMILY,
EDUCATION
AND
SOCIETY

THE FAMILY, EDUCATION AND SOCIETY

by

F. MUSGROVE

Professor of Research in Education,
University of Bradford

ROUTLEDGE & KEGAN PAUL
LONDON

First published 1966
by Routledge & Kegan Paul Limited
Broadway House, 68-74 Carter Lane
*London, E.C.*4

Printed in Great Britain by
The Alden Press Limited
Oxford

© *F. Musgrove* 1966

Second impression 1967
Third impression 1969

SBN 7100 1875 4

Contents

Contents

Tables

Acknowledgements

CHAPTER VI is based on material which the author has used in articles for *The British Journal of Educational Psychology*. He thanks the editors for permission to use the material in this book.

He also thanks G. H. Johnson Esq., B.Sc. and G. B. Miles Esq., M.A., for their help with the inquiries on which chapter six is based, and Dr. J. F. Morris of the University of Manchester for permission to quote from his unpublished doctoral thesis.

I

The Changing Parent: the Substitution of Influence for Power

THE ARGUMENT of this book in essence is this: that the family still exerts a powerful influence on the prospects, capacity for development, and life-chances of the young. Schools in general are remarkably ineffective in moderating the influence of family background, when such moderating influences are necessary. Our contemporary problem is less to buttress the influence of parents than to limit it. Conversely we have to learn how to make our schools so effective that they can make a real impact on all the young who are entrusted to them. These developments are necessary and desirable to enable the individual to achieve the fullest development of which he is capable; to further the cause of social justice by eliminating the influence of 'birth'; and to promote a more unified and cohesive society by using schools as a bridge from family life to a wide and diversified range of social contacts, involvements and experiences.

Discussion of the family naturally gives rise to strong, complicated and often contradictory feelings. The family has provided us with some of our most intense emotional experiences, and for this reason is a particularly difficult subject to examine in an intellectually objective manner. But we are fortunate today in having at our disposal a great deal of information about the modern family which has been carefully and systematically collected. There is not enough; we know more about the kinship systems of African and Oceanic tribes than we know about our own. But even in England the psychologists and, more recently, the sociologists have begun to produce factual evidence which is often surprising and in conflict with common-sense impressions.

This book is about the changing family, its relationship to outside educational agencies, and its function as an educational agency itself. Our prime concern is with the English family, but we draw on American research where this is relevant. Both the similarities and the contrasts with American experience are illuminating; and while it would be dangerous to assume that the American condition is invariably a guide to our own, it would be presumptuous, naïve and parochial to imagine that American explorations of human relationships tell us nothing about ourselves. And they have the advantage that they are abundant, technically expert and frequently more searching than English inquiries in the same field. Not only do the Americans know more in a systematic way about their own family system than we know about ours; they also know more about their schools as social institutions.

But it is not only from ignorance of our own society that we turn to work on America—or even tribal Africa. The family is a universal organization, everywhere it has educational functions, and in all societies it is intelligible only in its relationship with other social institutions. Too often in recent years the functions of the family have been interpreted in parochial terms. This may be a healthy reaction against the wide-sweeping studies of pioneer scholars like Westermarck and Briffault. The time may now be ripe for pulling together particular local studies. This book has no such high ambitions. But within its modest scope it may claim, perhaps, to be a preliminary essay in synthesis.

THE DECLINE OF PARENTAL POWER

One of the most remarkable social changes of the past century has been the substitution of parental influence for parental power. Throughout the advanced countries of the West the power of parents has been radically curtailed in law and the rights and interests of the child protected. The social and economic bases of the power of parents had been undermined in many sectors of European and American society long before the law restricted their authority. It is something of a paradox that the measures taken to protect the child, particularly compulsory education—a revolutionary invasion of parental rights—have helped parents to regain some measure of authority by reducing the child's capacity and opportunity for independent earnings.

We can see significant changes in the position of parents as early as the seventeenth century. The role of parents began to contract, and with it some of their power and authority. This change occurred in America as well as in Western Europe. Bailyn[1] has described the changing seventeenth-century family in America (and the significance of these changes for education), and has attributed developments there to the special circumstances of a society of migrants and frontiersmen. But similar changes in Europe at this time have been ascribed to changing economic organization and a maturing capitalist system. Whatever the causes, the fact of contracting parental power and functions at this time seems reasonably well established.

The family as an all-purpose social and economic organization was beginning to restrict the range of its services in seventeenth-century England: 'First among these (changes) was the gradual emergence of the arts of teaching and healing from the domestic or family sphere to a professional organization.'[2] In particular, the authority of mothers declined as domestic industries were superseded by large-scale capitalistic enterprises.

Women of the household might still, at times, find an important place in industrial management even in the later eighteenth century. The wives, sisters and daughters of the Darby family showed themselves able to exercise top management functions, when the need arose, in the Darby ironworks at Coalbrookdale. But in family undertakings of this size, the women of the household were ever less in evidence. 'Prominent among the many influences which conspired together to produce so rapid a decline in the physique, efficiency and morale of upper-class women (in the later seventeenth century), must be reckoned the spread of capitalistic organization of industry, which by the rapid growth of wealth made possible the idleness of growing numbers of women.'[3]

The classical Industrial Revolution of the nineteenth century merely accentuated trends in family life which were of long standing. The final eclipse of domestic industries and the increase in the non-domestic employment of children reduced the effective power of parents. In the new centres of industry parents were often appendages of their young children, relying heavily on their (independent) earnings. Parents of higher social rank, particularly self-made industrialists, were often uncertain in a changing social scene and needed specialist aid to induct their sons into the society of a rapidly changing Britain. Boarding schools multiplied to meet their needs. Even the technology which the uprising generation must learn could no longer be transmitted through a family tradition in the family works.

Different reasons have been given for the decline which also occurred in parental authority in America at this time. The children of immigrants often have an advantage over their parents who may be handicapped by old habits, values and skills which are irrelevant in the new environment. In the wide open spaces of a vast new continent the young can easily and early acquire land and establish themselves in independence of their parents. In American society the frontier had a similar function to the factory in England: it was a young person's sphere, a guarantee of power and independence for the young.

In a frontier society the family turned in upon itself. It limited its ancient involvements in the wider community; and to that extent the family lost its capacity and authority to introduce the child into the wider world of non-domestic concerns.

As the family contracted towards a nuclear core, as settlement and resettlement, especially on the frontier, destroyed what remained of stable community relations, and constant mobility and instability kept new ties from strengthening rapidly, the once elaborate interpenetration of family and community dissolved. The borderline between them grew sharper; and the passage of the child from family to society lost its ease, its naturalness, and became abrupt, deliberate, and decisive.[4]

Formal educational institutions were increasingly necessary to effect this deliberate transition.

The family in both England and America was forced by circumstances from its earlier social prominence and authority; it also seems to have staged a voluntary and deliberate withdrawal. Public authorities remarked on the declining significance of parents in the lives of their children (and of other people's children entrusted to them as apprentices); and they attempted to bolster up their failing authority. Within a decade of their founding, says Bailyn, all the American colonies passed laws 'demanding obedience from children and specifying penalties for contempt and abuse'. It was ruled in Connecticut and Massachusetts that nothing less than capital punishment should be visited on those guilty of filial disobedience. The head of a household should assert his authority over his children, servants and apprentices. Only the full exercise of paternal power could save the nation.

In the quite different circumstances of England similar complaints and exhortations were heard at the same time. The guilds promulgated regulations enjoining full exercise of authority upon the master and fitting docility upon his apprentice. Masters were ever more reluctant to assume power which involved commensurate responsibility.

The very protestations of paternal power by seventeenth-century social and political theorists are a measure of the father's declining authority. Those monarchists who attempted to justify royal autocracy as the exercise of absolute power by the father of a family, were uneasily aware that fathers were no longer absolute. Filmer in his *Patriarcha* (1680) maintained that 'the father of a family governs by no other laws than his own will, not by the laws and wills of his sons or servants. There is no nation that allows children any action or remedy for being unjustly governed.'

In France Bodin had argued similarly (in his *Six Books of the Commonwealth*) that 'in any right ordered society, that power of life and death over their children which belongs to them under the law of God and of nature, should be restored to parents'. But he knew that in fact he lived in other times, that 'Nowadays, fathers have been deprived of their paternal authority . . . it is now even suggested that a son can defend himself and resist by force any unjust attempt at coercion on the part of the father.'

It is true that the authority of the medieval king had rested in large measure on his position as a super-parent. Only he could interfere with the jurisdiction of parents in the interests of the children. (Vestiges of this royal power remain when children are made 'wards of Court'.) But by the later seventeenth century both the parent and the super-parent were diminished in authority. John Locke described the realities of contemporary royal and parental power. It was the realities of more modest paternal power and family pretensions in late-seventeenth-century England which provided him with arguments to refute Filmer's thesis. He maintained (in his *Second Treatise on Political Government*) both natural and divine rights for children 'not only to a bare subsistence, but to the conveniences and comforts of life as far as the condition of their parents can afford it'. Paternal authority was conditional: a man even other than the biological father could earn 'by paternal care, a title to proportionable degrees of paternal power'. Paternal authority was limited and specific, 'only for the help, instruction and preservation of their offspring. The paternal is a natural government, but not at all extending itself to the ends and jurisdictions of that which is political.'

Although the social and economic bases of parental power were being undermined in Europe from the seventeenth century onwards, the law was reluctant to bring itself into line with changing social realities. The fiction of paternal omnipotence was cherished. In England the state made no formal enactment to buttress failing parental power, but neither did it take any step to limit it until the closing decades of the nineteenth century. So reluctant was it to invade the privacy of family affairs that incest was not made a criminal offence until 1908. Until so late it was simply assumed— against overwhelming evidence—that (in the words of Bodin) 'The affection of parents for children is so strong, that the law has always presumed that they will only do those things which are of benefit and honour to their children.'

Historic and increasingly inappropriate assumptions regarding the inviolability of the family and the wide powers and discretion of the father have been maintained by English Common Law, which has tended to defend the rights of parents from the encroachments of public authorities. In the year 1883—just as, in fact, society was at last making decisive encroachments—Lord Justice Bowen, referring to the natural rights and duties of parents, observed (in the leading case of Re Agar Ellis):

> The Court must not be tempted to interfere with the natural order and course of family life, the very basis of which is the authority of the father, except it be in those very special cases in which the State is called upon, for reasons of urgency, to set aside parental authority and to intervene for itself. . . . To neglect the natural jurisdiction of the father over the child would be to set aside the whole course and order of nature . . . and would disturb the very foundation of family life.

The long arm of the state reached into the family with coercive power only at the end of the nineteenth century. With great reluctance Statute Law brought about a pro-found modification in the historic Common Law position of the father and the family. In the year of Lord Justice Bowen's judgement, society was organizing itself to invade the family: the first Society for the Prevention of Cruelty to Children was founded in Liverpool; in 1889 the N.S.P.C.C. was established; and in 1895 it obtained a Royal Charter.

Two Acts of Parliament sponsored by A. J. Mundella—the Education Act of 1880 and the 'Children's Charter' of 1889—gave the child legal protection against negligence and positive ill-treatment by parents. By the latter Act the courts were empowered to remove a child from home to a place of safety and to require the parents to contribute towards its upkeep. Later the police were empowered to remove a child from home even without a court order if cruelty was suspected; and in 1904 this right was extended to officers of the N.S.P.C.C. George Bernard Shaw appreciated the implications of these measures. In his preface to *Misalliance* (1910) he commented: 'There is a Society for the Prevention of Cruelty to Children which has effectually made an end of our belief that mothers are any more to be trusted than stepmothers, or fathers than slave drivers.'

Relics of an ancient paternal power remain. A father still has the right to the services of his infant children, and he may recover damages for the seduction of a daughter whose capacity for service is presumed to have been thereby impaired. A father has the right to the custody of his legitimate children, the right to determine the child's religion, education and where he shall live. But the antique structure of paternal authority has been dramatically undermined by twentieth-century legislation. Most notable of modern statutes is the Children and Young Persons Act of 1933 which gives the courts wide powers over young persons below the age of seventeen who are judged to be 'in need of care and protection'. Magistrates have the power to over-rule parental authority wherever this is falling short of what the magistrates consider to be 'proper care and guardianship'. A citadel which has remained inviolate throughout the centuries is now wide open to a vast army of children's officers, probation officers, education officers, and welfare officers of various kinds. The pretensions of centuries have been formally humbled in as many decades.[5]

THE INCREASE IN PARENTAL INFLUENCE

As the formal power of parents has declined their influence has increased. Yet it is commonly alleged that the influence of the modern family has diminished in two important respects. Parents, it is said, have less influence than formerly on the behaviour and moral standards of their children, particularly in their teens; and family connections are less important in securing special advantages for children as they embark on their careers. The decline of parental influence in the former sense is deplored; in the latter sense it is applauded as a prime requirement of a democratic society.

Both lamentation and applause are premature. Later chapters of this book examine in some detail the potency of the bond between parents and even their teenage children, and the persistent influence of family circumstances and connections on the life-chances of the young. In this introductory chapter the author will merely indicate some more general grounds for supposing that, with the rise of a more democratic and 'open' society, the influence of parents on their children's personal development and prospects has probably increased rather than diminished.

Studies of delinquency are largely responsible for the impression that the mid-twentieth-century family is failing to supply adequate moral guidance and is even promoting delinquency through psychologically harmful child–parent relationships. This emphasis on the defective family is not new. In the middle of the nineteenth century Mary Carpenter concluded from her wide experience that poverty was not a major cause of delinquency, but defective home management. She advocated the setting up of Reformatories in which dedicated men and women would 'stand in the parental relationship to such (mismanaged) families, a most arduous office, fraught with much greater difficulties than those which assail its natural guardians'.[6]

In 1925 Cyril Burt, in his *Young Delinquent*, gave 'defective discipline' in the home as a major cause of juvenile crime. Investigators with a psycho-analytical orientation have since probed the child–parent relationship more deeply and have seen 'delinquent susceptibility' arising from the parents' failure to lead the young child from the 'pleasure-pain' to the 'reality' principle.[7] The parent again assumes major responsibility in the eyes of those who see juvenile crime—particularly theft—as an outcome, in many cases, of an 'affectionless personality', starved in its first years of life of maternal affection.[8] Interpretations along these lines have helped to create the impression that the rising crime rate is a symptom of widespread family breakdown.

If the family were as defective as is popularly supposed, what would require explanation would be the low rates of juvenile crime. Historical trends in crime are notoriously difficult to establish; and while there has been an increase in convictions since the nineteen-thirties, there has quite certainly been a dramatic decrease in juvenile crime since Victorian or even Edwardian days. It is no longer possible to dismiss virtually the entire working-class population as 'the criminal classes' or the 'perishing and dangerous classes'. Social observers in Victorian Britain could speak of a large 'sunken' class and an even larger 'sinking' class. David Stow estimated in the middle of the century that a sixth of Glasgow's population belonged to the former and a third to the latter; that a half of the population was 'depressed and vicious'.[9]

Today at the peak period of delinquency (fourteen years) less than 3 per cent of the age group—despite the efficiency and zeal of the modern police—are convicted of indictable offences. Even if we double this figure to make allowance for those who are let off with a warning, for those who got away, and for those from white-collar homes who escape official penalties, we are concerned with only a tiny minority of families.

In many of these families there would have been seriously defective child–parent relationships if the child had *not* enjoyed an episode of delinquent activity. Subcultural interpretations of delinquency, notably by Cohen in America[10] and by Mays in England,[11] have shown that delinquents' behaviour may be a symptom of social and psychological adjustment rather than of maladjustment, even a sign of rude social health. If a family happens to be located in an area with a vigorous delinquent subculture (though it is possible, but unlikely, that delinquency-prone families don't just *happen* to be there), the children are likely as a matter of course to be inducted into its values and activities. It is the children who fail to make this adjustment to the predominant values of their immediate world who are probably in need of psychiatric treatment and whose parents need investigating for their maladaptive child-care practices.

It is probable that less than 5 per cent of juvenile criminals graduate to adult crime. Their capacity to adjust to the delinquent subculture is matched by their capacity to adjust to the requirements and controls of normal adult life when the time comes. And even those who proceed to adult crime are not necessarily the victims of a disturbed childhood and defective home. As a recent study of adult criminals has suggested:

> criminality is a normal aspect of the social structure, a permanent feature of any complex society, an ongoing social activity like the practice of medicine or police work or university teaching or stevedoring. It is sustained, like these other activities, by a subculture of people and groups most of whom are tolerably well adjusted to their subcultures and most of whose leaders are not only socially and personally competent but are also exceptionally able individuals.[12]

Indeed, their families might well be proud of them.

Some delinquents are doubtless in revolt against their parents, challenging them, or even testing out their love and loyalty. But in general young people in Britain today, whether delinquents or not, have little need to rebel against their parents or to test their only too patent concern and solicitude.

Young people in Britain today are strongly attached to their homes and appreciative of parental care. The National Association of Mixed Clubs and Girls Clubs published in

1960 a pamphlet entitled *Club Members Today*. The results of an inquiry into the attitudes of club members showed that there was no lack of affection between young people and their parents. Home still means a great deal to the young people of Britain.

It is possible that home means more than ever before. As the 'instrumental' functions of the family have diminished, its 'affective' or 'expressive' role (in Talcott Parsons' terms) has probably become more important. Recent inquiries conducted by the author (see Chapter VI) lend support to this view.

While investigators who have been concerned with specific problems of social breakdown have been impressed by the deficiencies of modern family life, others who have been concerned with the vast majority of normal families have been impressed by parental concern and competence. The Newsons, investigating child-rearing practices in Nottingham, gathered abundant evidence, from all social levels, of parental conscientiousness and concern.[13] In America, Bettelheim and Janowitz have observed (in discussing the possibilities of parental education to eliminate ethnic prejudice):

> In our society, an increasing number of parents are genuinely interested in problems of child rearing. The educator does not need to go after such parents, they seek him out if they have any hope that he will relieve their anxieties about whether they are bringing up their children properly and whether they are good parents.[14]

It is the popularizer of modern psychological theories who must carry a heavy weight of responsibility if family relationships go all awry. There is no doubt that a large and growing number of parents are his attentive pupils.

It seems likely that the 'open' society unleashes unsuspected parental energies. It is one of the paradoxes of the democratic state that precisely because the advantages and disadvantages of birth are to some extent eliminated—or thought to be eliminated—the potency of parents is enhanced. In a closed or caste society, with a fixed and rigid hierarchy, no amount of parental encouragement and pressure can secure for the child any improvement on the status to which he was born. By the same token, parents of higher social rank can rest assured that their children cannot fall below their own social level, however inadequate their upbringing and disastrous their education. Parental indifference is common when the future of the children is in any case predetermined.

It was a widespread complaint against the gentry of seventeenth- and eighteenth-century England that they neglected the upbringing and the education of their children, particularly the education of their eldest sons. Swift in his *Essay on Education* and Defoe in *The Compleat English Gentleman* rebuked the gentry on this score, pointing out that the boys were generally neglected at home, and that few eldest sons were sent to public schools or universities. To this charge the gentry replied: Why should we bother unduly with their education when their future is in any case assured?

In an open society the possibilities of downward mobility for their children galvanize high status parents into frenzied activity; and the lure of high status through achievement quickens the interest of low status parents in their children's educational progress and potential. An open, democratic society is an almost certain cure for parental unconcern. The danger is not that the child will be neglected by his parents, but that he can seldom escape their searching scrutiny and continuous appraisal. The children are fortunate if they escape being submerged under the latest and most expensive editions of the *Children's Encyclopaedia*.

In an open society which rewards merit and achievement, parents have every inducement to provide the setting and circumstances, the encouragement and exhortation, which are likely to lead to meritorious conduct. Parents grow in importance as social strategists, managers of the family's advance to social distinction. Today they become experts in educational strategy, since this is increasingly the key to success. When marriage was more important as a means of social advance, parents—particularly mothers—gained power and importance in the family as commanders-in-chief of matrimonial manoeuvres.

Careful and elaborate planning might be necessary to capture suitable suitors; and to minimize competition it was arranged that daughters 'came out' by seniority, and only when the one ahead had married. The novels of Jane Austen provide blue-prints for such maternal strategists. Mrs Bennet, it is true, did not fight according to the strictest conventions of the day: her younger daughters came out before the older ones had secured husbands; for, as her daughter Elizabeth pointed out to Lady Catherine de Bourgh, holding back the younger girls to prevent competition 'would not be very likely to promote sisterly affection and delicacy of mind'.

Marriage is by no means unimportant today as a means of social advance or, at least, of maintaining social status; and mothers may still gain considerable importance as stage-managers of appropriate encounters. But today parents are first and foremost experts in the technicalities of the educational system. Teachers may be ingenious in trying to disguise what really happens (in selecting, promoting and classifying children, for example); but parents are seldom deceived.

Increasingly parents are educational experts, making their views known to teachers, exerting pressures on the school to modify its procedures and curriculum, discouraging it from activities which are not career-oriented.

And they know that suitable social contacts for their children may be as important as educational certificates. The high and rising rates of geographical mobility in advanced Western countries are in considerable measure a symptom of parental concern. (Even oversea migration seems often to be undertaken less for the sake of a better job for father than for brighter prospects for the children.) But local moves in particular may be made to secure superior social contacts for the children in a better neighbourhood. Children's interests promote as yet unchartered circulations and eddies of population; parents have a new significance as prospectors of rewarding social territory.

The open society has given parents a new significance in their children's lives. Parents have been quick to realize their new importance; they have responded—even they have over-responded—to the challenge. Today there is point in their exertions. The danger is not that parents in general are failing to exert themselves on their children's behalf; but that their influence is all-pervasive and the child has no respite from parental concern.

II

Home and School: an Historic Conflict

A DANGEROUS INSTITUTION

THE SCHOOL has often been seen as a threat to the home in
at least two senses: in undermining parental influence and
family values and substituting the different and perhaps
quite alien influence of teachers; and in undermining parents'
sense of responsibility, taking on child-care duties which
should 'properly' belong to parents.

The school must always be at least a potential danger to
the family on both counts. But parents in the past, and perhaps some today, have also seen the school as a major
source of vice and serious moral contamination through the
undesirable and even depraved characters assembled there
to be taught. The well-to-do parent sending his son to Eton
in the eighteenth century would give careful instructions
about the friendships he should make and avoid; today the
careful mother may warn her child about getting in with
boys 'from the Estate'. She hopes at least to preserve his
accent if not his morals. So it is that the best laid schemes of
social mixing and 'integration' may be set at naught by
parental guidance and filial obedience.

So dangerous to the family have schools often appeared
that influential social observers in the past and even today
have been against spreading them. Most educational advances, like advances in other social services, have been
resisted on the grounds that they would 'undermine the
family'. Services previously performed by members of the
family for one another, however inadequately or even
dangerously, should not be undertaken by paid and 'soul-
less' professionals.

This argument has often been used for the gross exploitation of the goodwill which families usually have, up to a point, for their members. This exploitation can be seen in its most naked form in present-day tropical Africa, where services such as old-age pensions, free schooling, unemployment insurance and the like, may be withheld not only on the grounds of economy, but in order to sustain the family and keep its sense of responsibility unimpaired. Widows' pensions might seriously weaken a man's obligation and resolve to inherit the wives of his deceased brother.

The 'sanctity of the family' as an excuse for withholding more school education is of long standing. The argument has been used particularly effectively to prevent more extensive provision of schools for younger children (and also in recent years to justify the means test for university students). To the argument of sanctity has been added the argument of psychological health which stems principally from the writings of John Bowlby. The school, by breaking or weakening the link between the young child and its mother, becomes a broiler house of 'affectionless personalities'.

Long before they received the support of Dr Bowlby social and educational theorists objected to the setting up of schools for infants. Wilderspin, one of the pioneers of the infant school movement in the first half of the nineteenth century, was forced to argue strenuously throughout the many editions of his book, *The Infant System*, that his schools, if they were allowed to spread, would not really debauch the nation and relieve parents of all sense of duty.

Wilderspin knew that many would exclaim: 'Where are the natural guardians of the child? Where are its parents? Are we to encourage their neglect of duty, by becoming their substitutes?' But in early-nineteenth-century England Wilderspin knew that the choice was not between school and home, but between school and the streets, for the family had already demonstrated its incompetence: 'the child is deprived, during the whole of the day, of the controlling presence of a parent, and is exposed to all the poisonous contamination which the streets of the large cities afford.'

Even so enthusiastic an educationist as Sir James Kay-Shuttleworth, the first secretary of the Privy Council Committee on education, hoped that Infant Schools might not be needed indefinitely. When in 1862 he reviewed the history of these schools, which took children from the age of three, he applauded their success but looked forward to their disappearance in the future when parents, 'more lettered and less sensual, will be less prone to neglect infants and children of a riper age'.[1]

In the past quarter of a century nursery schools have often been opposed on the more psychological grounds that young children may be irreparably damaged if teachers are substituted to any extent for parents. The writings of Bowlby, Burlingham and Anna Freud[2] have led to a probably exaggerated view of the consequences of 'maternal deprivation'. Bowlby's theories have been subjected to a highly critical scrutiny by Barbara Wootton in her book, *Social Science and Social Pathology* (1959). The research methods in particular have been called into question. In the nature of the case, if we study the background only of institutionalized children, or of children referred for psychiatric treatment, we know nothing about 'the ones that got away'—those who may have suffered from the deprivation of a mother's love and affection but have since developed so satisfactorily that they have not ended up in an institution, court or clinic. Research which does not take these into account 'is on a par with trying to calculate the insurance premiums to be charged for fire risks by reference only to those houses which have actually caught fire'.

When we are thinking of nursery and infant schools, precisely what is meant by maternal deprivation needs to be made clear. It is probably true, as Bowlby claims, that it is 'now demonstrated that maternal care in infancy and early childhood is essential for mental health. This is a discovery comparable in magnitude to that of the role of vitamins in physical health.' But Bowlby's main concern was with the removal of young children altogether from their mothers when the family failed for whatever cause; and he claimed that the evidence was that bad homes are better than good institutions (though it may depend on just how bad the home and how good the institution). It would be a pity if the bogy of 'maternal deprivation' was made the excuse to limit the development of educational provision for a few hours a week for the 'pre-school' child.

THE DISGRACE OF SCHOOLING

To send a child to a nursery school today may be thought by some to reflect unfavourably on its family. The mother is seen as evading her proper responsibilities. By the same token it was formerly a disgrace to go to school at all. If you came from a decent, responsible and competent family, which could do all the things that proper families were supposed to do (from bread-baking and instruction in Euclid to abortion and minor surgery), a school was unnecessary. Only a severely defective family justified the exposure of children to the grave moral dangers and barbarities of school life, whether in a public, charity or national school.

The view that the extension of education, even for adolescents, is to the disgrace of parents, can still be found. In his *Notes Towards the Definition of Culture* (1948) T. S. Eliot sees nothing to the credit of parents in the progressive raising of the school leaving age.

> Instead of congratulating ourselves on our progress, whenever the school assumes another responsibility hitherto left to parents, we might do better to admit that we have arrived at a stage of civilization at which the family is irresponsible, or incompetent, or helpless; at which parents cannot be expected to train their children properly; at which many parents cannot afford to feed them properly, and would not know how, even if they had the means; and that Education must step in and make the best of a bad job.

To go to the first Sunday Schools was to bring discredit on one's parents. It was rather like attending an Approved School today. It suggested that parents had fallen down on their job and were handing over to other agencies. Hugh

Miller has described his early-nineteenth-century childhood in the care of his uncles (see *My Schools and Schoolmasters*). They regarded Sunday Schools 'as merely compensatory institutions, highly creditable to the teachers, but very discreditable indeed to the parents and the relatives of the taught; and so they of course never thought of sending us there'.

The 'good parent' was not the one who sent his child to school, but the one who did not. This was a very common view until well into the nineteenth century. Thomas Guthrie, a well-known philanthropist and social worker, and a governor of Heriot's school in Edinburgh in the mid-nineteenth century, has told how he actively discouraged parents whose homes were at all adequate from sending their children to school. Only the defective family need do so. Many well endowed schools, which might offer free boarding facilities, leaving scholarships and grants to pay apprenticeship premiums, were tempting parents who should know better and were quite able 'to train up their children as olive plants round the domestic table, and rear them within the tender, kind, holy and heaven-blessed circle of a domestic home. There are nursed those precious affections towards parents, brothers, sisters and smiling babes, which, for man's good in this life, and the wellbeing of society, are worth more than all the Greek and Roman lore.'[3]

In the ideal theory of many foremost educationists at the end of the eighteenth century schools at any social level were a symptom of the family's failure. They existed only for the benefit of incompetent parents or unusually recalcitrant children. Richard Lovell Edgeworth, David Williams and William Cobbett were perhaps the best known of a host of educational theorists (and practitioners) who at that time regarded schools, however famous, as (in Edgeworth's words) 'a general infirmary for mental disease, to which all desperate subjects are sent, as a last resource'.

Edgeworth and Williams urged parents to educate their children until they entered a university or one of the professions. Many well-to-do people tried the experiment, in some cases with remarkable success in terms of academic attainments. William Cobbett took a farm so that he could educate his children himself, basing the curriculum on the routine of the farm. Edgeworth followed closely on the model supplied by Rousseau in *Émile* (1762) in educating his own children. (He was not altogether pleased with the result. As he complained in his *Memoirs* (1821), his son had little capacity to get on with people, 'he had too little deference to others, and showed an invincible dislike of control'.) In his *Treatise on Education* (1774) David Williams looked forward to the time when men would be 'capable of presiding over their own families and educating their children; and render schools themselves unnecessary'.

'No man is in all respects capable of educating a child,' argued Williams, 'but the father of it.' In saying this he expressed a potent ideal if not a really widespread practice of his day. If parents found it too difficult to measure up to these ideal responsibilities, then, said the theorists of the day, other domestic solutions must be found. The scientist (and private tutor), Joseph Priestley, recommended in his *Observations on Education* (1788) that 'a number of gentlemen of fortune, whose sons are nearly of an equal age, and free from all tincture of vice, and are all provided with separate tutors (should) contrive to bring them often together, so as to perform certain exercises in common'.

Williams was likewise prepared to concede in his later writings (*Lectures on Education* (1789)) that 'several families . . . might associate, place the tutor in a position to receive the pupils in hours occupied at home; to accompany them on scientific and playful excursions; to lead them in litera-ture . . .'. Any stratagem was worth trying to keep the children at home and save them from school.

A MYTHICAL GOLDEN AGE

The school came into universal use for children of all social levels in the nineteenth century for a variety of reasons; but not least because families were in general unable to shoulder the educational tasks which were urged upon them. One should not, however, underestimate the lingering reluctance of upper and middle class parents to hand over to the schools. A proportion of children from these social levels which was by no means negligible received their education at home until the end of the century. The Taunton Commission on the endowed grammar schools, which reported in 1868, found that 11·6 per cent of the undergraduates at Oxford and Cambridge had come not from school but from private (domestic) tutors; thirty years later the Bryce Commission on secondary education found that 11·4 per cent had received such a prior education.

What is in doubt is not the potency and widespread acceptance of the domestic ideal of education in the past, but the effectiveness and competence with which it was implemented. Under the Elizabethan Statute of Apprentices the bourgeois home was the principal institution for technical education. By the early nineteenth century it was quite clear that, by and large, it could not cope with the new technical knowledge and that the skills it taught had been rendered obsolete by industrial change. Among the professional middle classes and the gentry it was clear that parents were too busy, too idle, too indifferent, or too incompetent to measure up to the educational tasks which were recommended by the moralists of the age.

It is nonsense to talk of the mid-twentieth-century family as somehow representing a decline from an earlier Golden Age of parental skill and responsibility in the arts of child rearing. Statements from the pulpit and the press that the modern family is in decline from a former state of excellence have been too widespread and frequent to require documentation. Academic sociologists have often presented or implied a similar diagnosis. Sometimes they seem to approve the 'decline', or at least to accept it as inevitable. Thus Wilson sees the work of the teacher today necessarily taking on more 'parental' duties, since the family is 'associationally in decline': 'Even the service-agency aspects of the family have declined now that more meals are consumed in schools and canteens, new materials have all but eliminated stitching and darning . . . .'[4]

Usually the contemporary 'decline' is measured from a remoter point in an indeterminate past (as in the quotation from T. S. Eliot which is given above). The American sociologist, Sorokin, would have us reverse the 'decline', retrieve the alleged virtues of a remoter, bygone age, restore to the family its former solidarity and continuity, and above all reinstate it as 'the cornerstone of a new creative social order'. He derides modern marriage as mere 'bedroom companionship', unequal to its historic and proper task of socializing the young.[5]

In fact the family in the past was commonly grudging and inept in the social training it afforded the young. Only a sentimental, romantic and grossly inaccurate reconstruction of the past could ascribe to the family in the past two or three centuries a harmony, solidarity and beneficent influence on the young which it is our duty to recapture. At whatever social level we look, the eighteenth- and nineteenth-century family was in urgent need of outside educational aid long before the Industrial Revolution produced its own special problems for family life (in the form of housing difficulties, urban concentration and migration). When the family was not negligent, incompetent or just tyrannical, it was commonly a terrible bore. The debilitating effects of protected, self-sufficing domesticity, the sheer boredom of life with virtually nobody else but father, can be seen particularly well in the memoirs and the novels which have come to us from the parsonages of the day (whether genially presided over by George Crabbe or less genially by Patrick Brontë). It was not only the Brontë children who were driven to writing novels in sheer self-defence against an overwhelming ennui. (Indeed, one young woman writer of the time, Maria Edgeworth, felt constrained to write a novel entitled *Ennui* to expose a prevalent malaise of her day.)

The virtues and effectiveness of the domestic training of apprentices at least in the eighteenth century have been exaggerated by historians. The neglect which was common in the households of the gentry and professional men has perhaps been obscured by the shining example of John Stuart Mill. The industrial training given to children by their parents in domestic industries or in factories and mines was often ruthless and savage in its methods and the basis of the gross exploitation of children's labour by their parents.

Few memoirs have been left by lower class persons describing their upbringing in the eighteenth century. In the next century this deficiency is to some extent offset by the reports of royal and other official commissions of inquiry into labour and social conditions, and also by the reports of free-lance investigators and of social workers. Two important memoirs of men born into relatively humble homes in the eighteenth century are provided by William Hutton and Thomas Holcroft. Holcroft's upbringing and 'training' at the hands of his father was as capricious as it was savage and uncomprehending. At the age of seven he was given an ass, instructions to buy coal from the mines and full responsibility for transporting and marketing it. Holcroft recalls that his father would beat him,

> pull my hair up by the roots, and drag me by the ears along the ground, till they ran with blood. . . . Yet probably within an hour after he had exercised his severity upon me, he would break out into passionate exclamations of fondness, alarming himself lest he should some time or other do me a serious mischief, and declaring that rather than do so, he would a thousand times prefer instant death.

Such father-tutors survived into the factory system. Family work-units infiltrated intact into the mines and early factories. The report of the Mines Commission of 1842 was full of instances of fathers (and other close relatives) grossly exploiting and abusing their own children. 'However incredible it may seem,' said one witness, 'yet I have taken evidence from fathers who have ruptured themselves from straining to lift coals on their children's backs.' This was often done as part of the 'training' involved in the twelve-year apprenticeship (from the age of nine) to which youngsters were frequently subjected. The system was likened to the African slave trade, and the slave dealers and masters were the fathers of the children involved.

The great achievement of the early Factory Acts (in the eighteen-thirties and forties) was not that they protected child workers from the owners, but from their fathers. The family work units were broken up (often as a by-product of the administration of the Acts), and the father lost his 'training' function with regard to his own children.

William Hutton's treatment at his father's hands differed from Thomas Holcroft's only in that the savagery was never interrupted by remorse. But his uncle, to whom he was apprenticed, was still more forbidding as a teacher. He beat the young man 'to that degree, and with an unmerciful broomstick of white hazel, that I thought he would have fractured my bones and dislocated my joints'. This was the 'extended family' in action as an educational institution. By the time he was eighteen Hutton found this savage training unbearable and, like many another apprentice of the age, ran away from a situation which was simply intolerable.

The condition of the upper- and middle-class family is much more fully documented. Those moralists who urged parents of this social level to shoulder their responsibilities, did so with good reason. The refusal of middle- and upper-class mothers to suckle their own infants, the universal use of wet nurses and the prolonged abandonment of babies to nursing mothers of the lowliest social station, was a scandal of the eighteenth century constantly ventilated by writers and preachers.

Well-to-do parents scarcely knew their children. They hired an army of parent-substitutes. As one experienced tutor to the gentry complained: 'The father's attention is divided by the mercenary politics of parties and the qualities of brutes; mothers are occupied by frivolous plans of fatiguing dissipation. . . . But of the children they know only their persons and reputation in the house.'[6] Children were banished to remote parts of the house and were more often in the stables than the schoolroom.

The late-eighteenth-century novelist, Clara Reeve, would have liked all children to receive their education at home, but had no faith in parents as she knew them. 'If all mothers fulfilled their duties,' she argued in her *Plans of Education* (1792), 'there would be little occasion for boarding schools; but if they give up their time and attention to dress, to visiting, to cards, to public places, it is better that the children should go to school, than that they should converse with servants, or play in the streets.'

The general indifference and incompetence of European gentry in the care of their children led the eighteenth-century philosopher, Helvétius, to propound the solution which eventually prevailed: the removal of children altogether from home to the care of the school. 'What mother, in fact, studies the education of her children, reads the best books on the subject, and endeavours to understand them?' he asked in his *Treatise on Man*. 'The degree of attention we pay to any affair, is a measure of the degree of solicitude we have for its success. Now if this rule be applied to the care of children, nothing will be found more rare than maternal love.'

The upper-class family of eighteenth-century England seems to have concentrated on three branches of teaching and beyond these to have been remarkably negligent in training the young. With quite ruthless efficiency young children were taught to read, to endure pain and to prepare for their probable early death. Considerable thought and effort were given to this teaching.

Mrs Wesley's methods of teaching her children to read are perhaps most widely known. (John Ruskin gives an account of similar 'resolutely consistent teaching' by his mother in his *Praeterita*.) When one of the Wesley children reached the age of five, a day was set aside to teach it to read. All in turn began their lesson at nine in the morning; by five o'clock they knew their letters, 'except Molly and Nancy, who were a day and a half before they knew them perfectly,' for which their mother thought them very dull. On the following day the child was ready to tackle the first chapter of Genesis.[7]

In the days before anaesthetics it was necessary to come to terms early with pain. Parents devised elaborate schemes for 'hardening' their children. They dipped them in icy well water; they crept up behind them and dropped molten sealing wax on their bare arms. (The latter was the practice of Edgeworth's friend, Thomas Day—author of *Sandford and Merton*—in rearing the orphans Lucretia and Sabrina.) Mrs Sherwood, author of children's stories, tells of a common practice, to which she was herself subjected.

> It was the fashion then for children to wear iron collars round the neck, with a backboard strapped over the shoulders: to one of these I was subjected from my sixth to my thirteenth year. It was put on in the morning, and seldom taken off till late in the evening; and I generally did all my lessons standing in stocks, with this stiff collar round my neck.[8]

A great output of enormously popular books, which ran through many editions, prepared children for an early death. Only about half the children born at any social level survived to the age of 15; and an average eldest child of this age would have seen three younger brothers and sisters die. Death could not be ignored. The subject was not taboo, as it has since become; it was indeed considered with relish. Education could not be conducted then as today on the assumption that we are all immortal. There was no elaborate institutional provision for hiding away the dead and the dying from the healthy and the living. In small houses with large families the corpse was a frequent bed companion.

For the child who had perhaps seen little of death at home the public scaffold was available to remedy the deficiency. Hangings were used by conscientious parents as salutary educational spectacles. Thomas Holcroft was suitably haunted through life by the hangings his father insisted on his seeing when he was nine. In her *Fairchild Family* Mrs Sherwood described a father taking his youngsters on an educational visit to a gibbet—an example for her readers to follow.

By the early nineteenth century the exposure of young children to all the circumstances of death was being questioned. Louisa Hoare's warning to upper-class parents foreshadows a change in attitude while indicating a still general practice. In her *Hints for the Improvement of Early Education* she says: 'Great care is required that children do not imbibe terrific and gloomy ideas of death, nor should they incautiously be taken to funerals, or allowed to see a corpse. On this point, books are often injudicious.' This injudicious literature had for long enjoyed a widespread popularity.

Stories which told of the holy lives and joyful deaths of children who died young were best sellers. The reader was spared no detail of death-bed anguish. Mostly written in the seventeenth century, apart from a final wave produced by and for the late-eighteenth-century Sunday Schools, they were in vogue until the end of the eighteenth century—in fact until the rates of child mortality began to decline and they lost much of their point. They were designed to be read by mothers to their very young children. Typical is Whitaker's book, *Comfort for Parents Mourning over their Hopeful Children that Dye Young* (1693). 'This may be the last month, or week, or day, that you have to live,' he tells his reader; 'as young as you are gone to the cold mansions of the grave, and what security have you?' He invited his young readers to 'go into the shops, and see if there be no coffins your size: go into the churchyard and see if there be no graves your length.' Stories of young children dying were very popular, as popular as twentieth-century horror-comics, but read with adult approval and guidance. William Godwin recalled in later life how, after reading these accounts (in particular Janeway's horrific *A Token for Children*), 'I felt as if I were willing to die with them. . . .'[9]

But the broad picture of child-rearing in eighteenth- and nineteenth-century England at all social levels is one of general inadequacy. The campaign which drew much of its authority from Rousseau and was vigorously prosecuted by

such as Edgeworth, Day, Williams and Mrs Sherwood undoubtedly had considerable effect in recalling many upper-
class parents to a perhaps exaggerated view of their duties
between the seventeen-sixties and the eighteen-thirties.
Books were written to help them, like Edgeworth's *Practical
Education* and George Chapman's *Treatise on Education* (1790);
but many converted parents were over-ambitious and their
first enthusiasm to be tutors to their children soon flagged.
James Mill was probably untypical in his efficiency. More
often, those parents who decided to take their educational
function seriously were dilatory and unsystematic. Like
Edmund Gosse's father in the eighteen-fifties, they educated
their children 'cheerfully, by fits and starts'. (Herbert
Spencer enjoyed similar desultory home tuition.) By the
eighteen-thirties, when the reformed public schools and the
new proprietary schools were offering their services, middle-
class parents were only too happy, in general, to hand their
sons over.

The working-class family was in even more urgent need
of aid. A high and probably growing proportion of working-
class children were beyond the control of home, factory or
school until compulsory education in the eighteen-seventies
and eighties swept them from the streets. This was not
simply a feature of the new urban life under the Industrial
Revolution. The poet Cowper had described such scenes in
rural Buckinghamshire in the eighteenth century, 'where
children of seven years of age infest the streets every evening
with curses, and with songs to which it would be unseemly
to give their proper epithet'.[10]

The Reformatory and Ragged Schools of the mid-
nineteenth century did something to civilize the great army
of children wholly beyond parental control. These children
were neither at school nor at work. It is a mistake to think
of children in the nineteenth century swept wholesale into
factories from which the schools eventually rescued them.
In Manchester in the eighteen-sixties, of children between
the ages of 3 and 12 (the age of school attendance), some
6 per cent were at work, 40 per cent were at school, but 54

per cent were neither at school nor at work. The majority were on the streets.

The Ragged Schools often improved the situation. Before schools of this type were established in Edinburgh, the streets 'swarmed with boys and girls whose trade was begging and whose end was jail. They rose every morning from the lower districts, like a cloud of mosquitoes from a marsh, to disperse themselves over the city and its suburbs.'[11]

At the lower levels of society the family had lost control. The school came to its aid. The establishment of elementary schools in the nineteenth century was a great sanitary operation, a gigantic street-clearing device. Compulsory schooling did not 'usurp' the parent; he had long been usurped by the street gang.

With the aid of the school the family has made remarkable progress over the past century in reclaiming the children. An old competitor has proved an effective ally. The school has not 'undermined' parents; it has strengthened them. The family as an all-purpose social institution had demonstrated its inadequacy long before the advent of compulsory education. With its diminished or at least shared responsibilities, it has been able to concentrate on a narrower range of services which are effectively within its grasp.

III

Success Story

A VARIETY of contemporary circumstances is alleged to have 'undermined' the family: geographical migration; social mobility; the social services; the rapidity of social change which gives children an advantage over their parents and places them in a new world which their parents scarcely understand. In consequence, it is claimed, the modern family is unstable and without authority.

In fact the modern family is our most successful social institution. Geographical migration and the social services have given it a new importance and have promoted its unity; social mobility (children rising above the social level of their parents) has not been shown to weaken the cohesion of the family or seriously to impair the bonds between parents and their prospering children; young people were seldom so deeply embedded in their families, particularly in the middle class; and as education becomes ever more protracted for more people, the prolonged dependence of the young into adult years is likely to become a marked feature of life at all social levels.

If parents have in some sense lost their authority (in a legal sense this is certainly the case), in general they were never so concerned, responsible and unsparing of themselves in the care of the young and consideration for the old. Within the family circle personal relationships were probably never more humane, equal co-operation never more apparent (and sexual relationships between husband and wife never more enjoyable now that the consequence is not the wife's eternal pregnancy). If the family is at all in danger, the threat comes from the least expected quarter: from wives rather than husbands, from mothers rather than children.

It is true that a hard core of problem families still neglect or actually ill-treat their children. But gone are the dark Victorian days when child insurance offered a hard cash inducement to impoverished parents to neglect their children out of existence. The child was scarcely born before the parents began to think of, if not actually to plot, its death.

In 1900 the N.S.P.C.C. instituted 3,226 prosecutions for ill-treatment and neglect. The decline in prosecutions in the twentieth century has been dramatic. In 1920 there were 1,533; in the years immediately after the Second World War there were somewhat under a thousand a year. The number has fallen steadily and continuously. In the year 1961–2 there were 418 prosecutions. This is only 12 per cent of the figure for 1900; but over these years the population has risen by 30 per cent.

There remains nevertheless an obstinate fringe of inadequate or even vicious parents. The total number of cases dealt with, but not necessarily leading to prosecution, has shown comparatively little change and has been running recently at some 40,000 a year. During the past decade there have been some eight cases per 10,000 of population per annum; in the previous 70 years the average rate was approximately nine per 10,000 of population. Today the great majority can be dealt with by warning and advice. (In 1889 the N.S.P.C.C. had to prosecute for cruelty and neglect in 33·3 per cent of cases; today in only 1 per cent.) But 40,000 cases involve upwards of 100,000 children under the age of fifteen, some 1 per cent of the population at risk. Forty thousand cases are 40,000 too many. But the problem, however difficult and unsavoury, is a marginal one. The twentieth century has undoubtedly seen a remarkable overall improvement in family relationships and a striking reduction in the proportion of criminally barbarous parents.

A POPULAR INSTITUTION

Far from being regarded as outmoded, an antique survival out of keeping with the new morality, the family was never more popular, marriage never more eagerly supported, particularly by the young. Those whose first (or even second or third) marriage has come to an end for whatever cause are usually eager to try it again, particularly the men. (Thus slightly more than three-quarters of divorced men re-marry, rather less than three-quarters of divorced women.) The problem is not that marriage and the family are unstable, but that they show perhaps an inappropriate rigidity.

Since 1911 marriage has enjoyed a popularity which was without precedent in Victorian England, although it may have been equalled at the end of the eighteenth and the beginning of the nineteenth centuries. Between 1785 and 1805 the marriage rate was over 17 per 1,000 of population;[1] rates in excess of this were not reached again until 1936–40 (19·2) and 1946–50 (17·7).[2] The late eighteenth century was a time of intense domesticity, with high marriage rates, particularly among the young, and high fertility. For this reason the late eighteenth century has been described by Carr-Saunders (in his *Population*, 1925) as 'an almost, if not quite, unique epoch in the history of the human race'.

There was less marriage in Victorian England than before or since. In particular there was less marriage among people in their early twenties. Between 1871 and 1911 the proportion of married men aged 20 to 24 declined by 38·6 per cent; the proportion of women by 30 per cent; but the proportion of married men in this age group rose by 66·4 per cent between 1911 and 1951; the corresponding increase for women has been 100 per cent. The nineteen-thirties in particular saw a remarkable change for young women: in 1931, while only 25·8 per cent of women aged 20 to 24 were married, by 1939, 34·4 per cent were married—an increase of one-third in eight years.[3]

At a time when sex was never so generally available—at least uncommercially—outside marriage, the institution of

33

marriage was never so strongly supported. But the eagerness of the young to enter into marriage is matched, it is said, only by their readiness to abandon it. It is true that there is a slight long-term tendency for early marriages to break down more often than marriages contracted in later years. (By definition, of course, they have had a longer period in which to be subjected to strain.) But the fact remains that in marriages of more than twenty years' standing the divorce rate is more than twice the rate prevailing in marriages of four years' standing or less. About 60 per cent of divorces occur in marriages which have lasted ten years or more. In view of the difficulties opposed by society to young marriage—not least the appalling and dispiriting problem of housing—the remarkable fact is not the instability of youthful marriages but their resilience.

The illegitimacy rate among young girls today is often taken as an indication that marriage and the family have fallen from an earlier state of grace, particularly with the young. Nobody who has studied the problem of bastardy in the eighteenth and nineteenth centuries, and the operations of the Poor Law authorities in forcing young men to marry pregnant girls, often with disastrous consequences for family life and the care of the young, would bewail contemporary morals. Measures taken under the Poor Law appear to have aggravated the very problems they were intended to solve. As the commissioners on the Poor Laws complained in 1834: 'The most active inducement to incontinence in the female is the prospect of all being cared for by a forced marriage, the usual consequence of a state of pregnancy in country parishes. Accordingly . . . it is found that the female in very many cases becomes the corruptor; and boys, much under the age of 20, are converted by this process into husbands.' Today young men who get girls into trouble seem to need little encouragement to marry them. Seventy per cent of girls under twenty who are 'in trouble' marry before the baby is born. Only 10 per cent of single women similarly troubled in their thirties secure a husband before the birth of the child.

Illegitimacy rates have indeed risen since the nineteen-thirties; but it is not the young so much as their seniors who are prone to give birth outside the bonds of wedlock. Only 1 per cent of single girls aged 15 to 19 had illegitimate babies in 1962, but 5 per cent of single women in their late twenties and early thirties did so. Of course there are fewer single women in their late twenties and early thirties than there are single teenage girls, and the lower rates of illegitimate births among the latter result in a larger number of babies (about a quarter of all illegitimate births).

There is no foundation in fact for present-day lamentations that marriage is less stable and its sanctity less regarded than in the past. There has, of course, been a great increase in divorce during this century; today married couples seek to end their marriages at the rate of some twenty to thirty thousand a year. But in view of the removal of obstacles to divorce over the past century (obstacles of a financial, social and legal kind), the spread of divorce cannot be regarded as a sign of increasing marital breakdown.

And divorce may occur today where death previously made it unnecessary. Even the high divorce rates in America have not resulted in higher breakdown rates, *from all causes*, over the past century. In the eighteen-sixties there were more than 30 dissolutions per 1,000 American marriages, today only 27.[4] And death, a major solvent of young marriages in the past, was less discriminating than divorce, striking the parent-couple equally with the childless. There can be little doubt that the massive substitution of divorce for death has been a major gain for modern family life.

There has been a fifty-fold increase in petitions for divorce over a hundred years. The increase has not been steady and continuous. 'Exceptional rates' must be ascribed to two major wars which saw a high rate of breakdown not only in war-time marriages but in marriages of long standing. Since the end of the Second World War divorce rates have been subsiding, settling to a more 'normal' level. Of marriages contracted 1939–40, 4·2 per cent had ended in divorce ten years later; but of marriages contracted 1944–5, war-time marriages too, only 3·8 per cent were ended by divorce over the next ten years.

The Matrimonial Causes Act of 1923 allowed wives, like their husbands, to petition on the grounds of adultery. (Herbert's Matrimonial Causes Act of 1937 made divorce possible for offences other than adultery, such as cruelty.) Over this period aid has been provided for people of limited means to obtain divorce. Of couples married 1921–2, who have enjoyed all these advantages, only 2·8 per cent were divorced thirty years later. This proportion increased for marriages entered into later in the twenties: it was 3·7 per cent for marriages contracted 1924–5.[5]

The rate for post-war marriages seems to be settling at some 5 per cent over thirty years. A 95 per cent survival rate—even a 90 per cent survival rate—is probably too high. (Of course an unknown proportion of marriages also end in separation, but even so the breakdown rate is marginal, even if these equal the number of divorces.) The persistence of an overwhelming majority of marriages probably indicates a high degree of social rigidity and personal inflexibility.

There is a strong case for making divorce more difficult and perhaps impossible for couples with dependent children; otherwise to make it possible by consent. The persistence of the great majority of marriages can be regarded as a failure to adapt to changing social and personal circumstances. At 40 most wives nowadays have their children launched into the world. They have retired. But their husbands still have more than twenty years to go. They could in many cases with profit to themselves and the community embark on non-domestic careers; their husbands (probably more naturally domestic than their wives in any case) might start a second family. Our present arrangements are appropriate to a social system which wore out its women by 40 with domestic drudgery and constant child-bearing, and offered them no satisfactory alternative employment.

A NEW DOMESTIC SERVICE

The modern family specializes in affection. It can do this job precisely because it need do little else. Sociologists who have predicted its decline have done so on the grounds that many of its historic tasks were being taken over by other institutions. Sprott has summarized these arguments in his *Sociology*:

> The family, under Western cultural conditions, has shrunk functionally. . . . Not so very long ago the household was almost self-supporting, providing its food and clothing, and its own social services. . . . Gradually, however, the state has undertaken to provide pre-natal attention, kindergarten schools, infant schools, and other forms of education; expanded medical services are available; the factory and the office provide the place of work . . . clubs and youth associations cater for the individual members of the household so that a new anti-family note is struck.

When the family has difficult and exacting tasks to perform, relationships within it tend to be characterized by formality and constraint...as in any other social group facing difficulties. It organizes itself along authoritarian lines, with a clear division of labour and chain of command; modes of address become formal, and husband and wife address each other by their surnames. Today the family as a work group is uncommon, running perhaps a shop or a farm. In such cases it tends to be less 'democratic'. (There is a good deal of evidence from America that farmers and their wives are much more autocratic than urban parents.[6]) Even the more typical 'companionship family' of today will turn temporarily into an autocracy when it mobilizes itself for some major operation like the annual continental holiday. An unaccustomed edge will creep into father's (or perhaps mother's) voice; one parent or older child will emerge as deputy head of the household and transmit orders until all the arrangements have been made and democracy can break out again when all are safely on the boat.

Homans, in his important book, *The Human Group*, has illustrated such changes in group relationships in industrial work groups, street-corner gangs, and the family of Polynesian Tikopia. Faced with a difficult environment the Tikopia family is organized under the command of the father. The father suffers in consequence. 'At best one's attitude (towards him) is admiration; at worst it is open hatred; its norm is respect.' But when individuals co-operate as equals, without one giving orders or taking the initiative more often than another, unbuttoned good fellowship and informality result. Brothers in Tikopia enjoy such a relationship.

The fact that parents and children have become friends in Western society is a symptom of the family's shrunken importance. Even husband and wife are pals in a manner which is without precedent and would have been considered unmanly and highly abnormal in husbands at any previous time in our history. The family can provide friendship because it has few demanding jobs, as a family, to do. And the evidence is that it provides friendship and affection generously and on an unprecedented scale. Children—even teenage children—look with remarkable kindliness on their parents, particularly their mothers. The vast majority of them are full of approval and appreciation. These are the conclusions from the author's research. There is no evidence that in general the young are filled with the resentment, contempt and hostility towards them which is frequently alleged.[7]

Neither are the old within the family circle denied care and affection. It is not only the 'nuclear' family (see page 40) which is in good heart, but the 'extended' family too. This is the conclusion which comes clearly out of much recent research, particularly the painstaking work of Townsend reported in his book, *The Family Life of Old People*. In working-class Bethnal Green in the nineteen-fifties old people were in close contact with their kin, receiving companionship and aid, and in turn rendering a variety of valued services, particularly in the care of grandchildren.

Ten per cent of the old people were 'isolated', with three or fewer social contacts a day. (But they were not necessarily neglected. Some had no kin within reach or no close relatives still alive.) On average the old people investigated had thirteen relatives living within a mile, and they saw three-quarters of all their children, both married and unmarried, once a week, as many as a third of them every day. Old people were getting a good deal of help both regularly and in emergencies, particularly from their female relatives.

In middle-class Woodford the picture is surprisingly similar. Although here the 'immediate family'—the married couple with dependent children—is much more on its own and less involved in relationships with kinsfolk, old people are in fact no more isolated and no less helped by their families than in Bethnal Green.

Young middle-class couples are commonly on their own. But when they reach middle age and their parents old age, the two generations often come together again. In retirement the old people may move to be with or near their children. In Bethnal Green the generations are together throughout life; in Woodford they separate when the children marry, but come together again when the parents grow old.

There are social-class differences in the 'life-cycle' of kinship, but neither cycle neglects the old. Willmott and Young have reported their inquiries into suburban middle-class life in *Family and Class in a London Suburb* (1960). 'Kinship may mean less in the suburb at other stages of life, but in old age, when the need arises, the family is once again the main source of support. The old felt that they could call on their children, the children that they *should* respond. . . . This sense of filial duty is as strong in one district as another.'

The conclusion of Townsend's research is quite clear. 'Widespread fears of the breakdown of family loyalties and of married children's negligence seem to have no general basis in fact.' The evidence is that 'the extended family is slowly adjusting to new circumstances, not disintegrating.

To the old person as much as to the young it seems to be the supreme comfort and support.'

The terms 'extended family' and 'nuclear family' are often used imprecisely and ambiguously by contemporary sociologists. The terms 'nuclear family', 'immediate family' and 'family of marriage' (as opposed to the 'family of origin' from which a spouse comes) are often used interchangeably, and with reference to modern urban, industrialized societies of the West this use is usually justified. The nuclear family is to be distinguished from the 'extended family' by the limited range of kin to whom it recognizes obligations. It consists of two generations only, the married couple and their unmarried children living together in one household. Ties between the parents and their (unmarried) children take precedence over all other kinship relationships. While it provides economic support for dependent children, it calls in paid specialists to provide many important services in the spheres of health, protection, education and recreation. One of its salient features is its non-authoritarian character, the generally democratic relationships within it. It is the nuclear family which Burgess and Locke refer to (in *The Family*, 1950) as the 'companionship family'. They see its main features as freedom in choosing a mate; the independence of the young marrieds of their parents; equality between husband and wife; increasing participation by the children in decision-taking as they get older; and the maximum freedom for individual members consistent with the achieving of family objectives.

The obligations recognized by the extended family embrace a wider and deeper range of kinsfolk. Strong bonds are retained with parents after marriage, and even their authority may be recognized. The classical model as found in traditional agricultural societies was characterized by its hierarchical and authoritarian structure and its geographical compactness. It was held together by binding reciprocal obligations and services. The extended family in its classical form has been seen by social scientists and philosophers as a hindrance to progress and social justice. It ties people down when economic advance may require a good deal of spatial movement; it provides rudimentary social services and so tends to delay the development of efficient and professional services; it subordinates the individual to the family; it does not foster the growth of school education chiefly because a man's prospects in life are determined less by his schooling than by his family connections and obligations.

Today the term 'extended family' may be used simply to describe the wider family without any suggestion that it is hierarchical and authoritarian or even geographically compact. The American sociologist, Litwak, whose research is discussed below, uses the term to describe a series of scattered nuclear families which are linked together on a footing of equality.

In his *Family Life of Old People* Townsend insists that the units of the extended family must be physically close if not actually in the same household. 'The relatives in the extended family are distributed over a number of households held together by common services and activities that go on among and between them.' Relatives live in one, two or more households, usually in a single locality, and see each other every day or nearly every day.

'Extended family' often means in contemporary sociological literature little more than independent nuclear (or 'conjugal') families more or less loosely linked, perhaps providing limited aid, and showing corporate action at deaths, births and marriages. Much research in America and Britain has shown that the extended family, in this rather loose sense, still exists and has reality for its members.

Although Townsend and Willmott and Young have shown that in contemporary Britain, in middle-class as well as working-class areas, the nuclear or conjugal family still recognizes obligations to the wider, extended family of which it is part, there remains, nevertheless, under our Western system of kinship and marriage, an inevitable tension and potential conflict between the interests of the immediate family and the extended family. On the whole we seem able to contain it because the extended family of Western society is not *too* extended; and because the aid required is usually marginal and rarely total—the social services bear the main burden of supporting the old and the sick and educating the young. Marginal aid may be gladly given when total aid would be withheld—it would be too serious a threat to the welfare of the immediate family. (Kinship aid *supplements* aid from the social services, as Townsend found: 'old people with daughters and other female relatives living near them make least claim on health and welfare services', but 'isolated people make dispro-portionately heavy claims'.) In this sense the social services prevent rather than promote the breakup of the extended family as a mutual aid organization.

When the extended family is really extensive, and when the aid it may claim is really onerous, in sheer self defence the Western-type nuclear family may have to sever its links with wider kin. This is seen most clearly in tropical Africa, where Western-style suburban families may be crushed if traditional kinship obligations are recognized and met. Thus among the educated class in Lagos, the more limited con-ception of the family which obtains in the West may have a strong appeal: 'For them, the mutual obligations of the family group have become a system of patronage, and they may be glad to escape from it into the seclusion of a private domestic life.' Such an escape may be a condition of survival as an urban, middle-class family; for:

> As men are promoted to the senior ranks of the civil service and commercial firms, they find themselves no longer contributors towards a mutual exchange of gifts and services, but the victims of demands which may be beyond their means: to their country cousins their wealth seems almost inexhaustible. Faced with insistent, even predatory claims, they may begin to restrict the range of relatives to whom they recognize an obligation.[8]

In England the nuclear family faces less exorbitant de-mands from a narrower circle of kin. In middle life a couple are likely to recognize claims only from their own children and parents. The extended family is not really very extensive. English people are unlikely to know the names of more distant relatives than uncles, aunts and first cousins. In Banbury, as Margaret Stacey reports in her book, *Tradition and Change* (1960), they have little knowledge even of their grandparents. They know the Christian names of some two-thirds of their paternal uncles and aunts, of four-fifths of their maternal uncles and aunts. The extended family is shallow and narrow. Even the comparatively strong bond between siblings tends to languish once the parents have died.

The extended family in England is doubtless a going concern and a valuable mutual aid organization; but the family is not really very extended, and the aid and support are given within comparatively circumscribed limits. In particular in-laws are little known compared with blood relatives and have comparatively little claim to support when in difficulties. A wife will help her mother and father but does not expect her husband to do so. (Townsend found that this was often the case.) While it is important to recognize that the English family has not 'disintegrated', it is absurd to see it as a substitute for a fully developed system of social services.

RESILIENT BONDS

Modern urbanization, social mobility and geographical migration have been supposed by sociologists to threaten family ties particularly in the extended kinship network. It is true, of course, that the modern Western family, particularly the middle-class family, expects and even encourages its children to leave home, and the neighbourhood of home, by the age of 18 to 20. The French sociologist, Le Play, thought in the early nineteenth century that the upper-class English family had moved further in this direction than continental families:

> The fathers of families on the continent associate during their life time with their heirs and thus train them by example

in the practice of the best traditions of the family. In England the heir of a rich family leaves the paternal home by or before the time of his marriage and except for temporary visits re-enters it only after the death of the father and the departure of the widow. The custom of cohabitation of the father and of the heir was no longer practised in England at the end of the eighteenth century.

By the end of the nineteenth century Émile Durkheim, when writing his celebrated study of suicide, saw this condition as general throughout Europe. Compared with the earlier ideal which Le Play implies, the family was certainly unstable. The modern family is in process of dissolution from the moment of its inception. Durkheim wrote:

> While it (the family) once kept most of its members within its orbit from birth to death and formed a compact mass, its duration is now brief. It is barely formed before it begins to disperse. Yet nothing can stop the movement . . . the individuals inevitably disperse in accordance with their ambitions and to further their interests into the wider spaces now open to them. No scheme can therefore offset this inevitable swarming of the bees and restore the indivisibility which was once the family's strength.

This dispersal certainly occurs, almost certainly with a greater intensity and range at higher social levels (as the author has argued in his study, *The Migratory Elite*). But the damage to kinship bonds is probably less than sociologists such as Talcott Parsons, for instance, once supposed. A democratic and industrialized society, maintained Parsons, requires that the individual be free to rise above his father (and his brothers) in the occupational (social) scale, and to migrate in search of opportunity. He must be 'free from hampering ties', and the result must be 'the segregation of his own family of procreation from those of his brothers'. His freedom of movement 'would not be possible if it (his family) were not an isolated conjugal family . . .'.[9]

Recent research in America, and to some extent in England, has not established the isolation of the mobile family.

Certainly urbanization *in itself* does not seem to reduce the importance of kinsfolk. Recent investigations in four major social areas of San Francisco have established that, 'compared to neighbours and co-workers, kin are generally more important in each neighbourhood by all the measures of informal participation used'.[10]

The geographical migration which is such a marked feature of the advanced industrial nations—we are all nomads now—may actually strengthen rather than weaken the extended family, though of course by dispersing it, it inevitably reduces the frequency of face-to-face contacts among its members. The dispersed units may become important contacts and staging posts for other migrant kinsmen. Even half-forgotten second cousins may be good for a bed, uncles and brothers for more substantial support. Before moving to take up a new job in a new area, contact will be established with even quite distant kinsfolk in the district who will provide emotional, social and conceivably economic aid, particularly during the actual crisis of movement. In a migrant society it pays to maintain contacts with scattered kinsfolk rather than allow distance to destroy them.[11]

Family bonds survive social mobility too, perhaps particularly easily in the urban setting. Research in Buffalo has shown that rising socially by no means destroys relationships with kinsfolk who have been left behind. The individual who has got on in life may set great store by his contacts with his less fortunate relatives. He values and enjoys their admiration and respect (and probably relishes their envy). In the anonymous life of the city he can keep their visits separate from those of his socially elevated friends. In Buffalo the social relationships of 920 married women were investigated in 1952. When women with available relatives in the area were compared, those who had risen in the social scale—even those who had very markedly bettered themselves—were found to receive more family visits a week than those who had not.[12]

It is possible that the family contacts of (mobile) women

are stronger than those of men. In their inquiries in Woodford, Willmott and Young found no evidence of widespread
destruction of family ties by social mobility, but the ties of
mobile women were more resilient than those of the men
who had got on in life. Mobile married women saw their
mothers and fathers as often as social stationaries; mobile
men saw their mothers as often, but their fathers less. The
only effect of social mobility appeared to be some reduction
of contact between men and their fathers; but the statistical
evidence for these conclusions, as the research team emphasized, is slight. But when the inquiries conducted in America
and England are put together, they support one another in
showing the capacity of the modern family to survive the
strains imposed by mobility in advanced, democratic,
industrial and urbanized societies.

DEPENDENT YOUNG

The speed of modern social change has been alleged to
detach young people from their parents. This has been
argued particularly by American social scientists like David
Riesman and Margaret Mead. Instead of bowing to the
authority of their elders, says Riesman in *The Lonely Crowd*
(1950), in contemporary 'other-directed' society the young
must acquit themselves before a jury of their peers.

Margaret Mead reaches a similar conclusion and maintains
that the speed of social change has undermined parents.
'Our system (of transmitting our culture through parents)
might work smoothly in a culture which was changing very
slowly. For an essential element in the system is that the
child is expected to take the parent as a model for his own
life style. In periods of rapid change, and especially when
these are accompanied by migrations and political revolu-
tions, this requirement of the system is unattainable. The
child will never be, as an adult, a member of the same culture
of which the father stands as the representative during his
early years.' In consequence, 'the socializing function of the
age group becomes very much intensified.' 'The surrogates

who carry the cultural standards have changed. They are no longer the parents, omnipotent and belonging to another order of being, but one's everyday companions . . .'.[13]

What is depressing is the extent to which Riesman and Mead are wrong. A great deal of research has been carried out in the last decade to test the truth of these views; and it shows them to be substantially in error. The influence of parents on the standards, values and behaviour of their children (even in their teens) is, in general, supreme. There is no really effective competitor—neither the age group nor, most serious of all, the school. Indeed, the claims of schools to have a serious impact on children's 'characters' are probably extravagant and unfounded. In general they are of negligible influence.

The comparative unimportance of the peer group in England has been indicated by Morris,[14] in France by Pitts,[15] and in America by Lucas and Horrocks,[16] Riley and Moore,[17] and Havighurst and Peck.[18]

In his inquiries among English secondary modern and grammar school pupils Morris found no slavish conformity to friends. He found that the proportion of adolescents who felt that they *should* support their friends in certain situations of conflict with adults 'declined sharply with age'. (On the other hand, the proportion who thought they would, in fact, support their friends remained relatively constant.) 'With the decline of reliance on authority comes the judgement that one should not lean too heavily upon friends. Many of the responses show a lively awareness of the shortcomings of friends as guides to conduct.'[19]

In France Pitts found the influence of the middle-class family unimpaired by schools or by peers. Children 'find their playmates more frequently among their siblings, each family living as a sort of separate society behind its high walls and closed shutters . . .'. 'One rarely hears in France of loyalty to the school peer group pushed to heroic levels when the group comes into conflict with adult values.'

Even in America the picture of the rejection of parents in

47

favour of peers is by no means supported in the extensive investigations of social psychologists. Lucas and Horrocks investigated the psychological needs of 725 adolescents at school in a small Ohio city. They were unable to discover a general need for 'peer group conformity'. But they did find a specific psychological need to conform to the expectations of adults.

In 1952, Riley and Moore investigated the values of 2,500 (mainly middle class) high school pupils who were given descriptions of twenty different 'personality models', some describing young people with a predominant desire for achievement, others describing young people who were first and foremost concerned to maintain good relations with their friends, and others describing young people chiefly interested in having a 'good time'. They indicated the models they would like to resemble, and those they thought their parents on the one hand, and their friends on the other, would prefer them to be like.

Their own self-preferences by no means coincided with what they thought their friends approved. Thus, while only 48 per cent thought their friends wanted them to resemble the 'success model', 67 per cent wanted to resemble it, and 80 per cent thought that this was what their parents wanted. Measured in this way, they were closer to their parents than their peers.

The young people of 'Prairie City' were intensively studied by Peck, Havighurst and their colleagues between the ages of 10 and 17 over the years 1943 to 1950. Friends, teachers and school subjects made a negligible impact on their socio-moral values compared with parents, particularly mothers. (We delude ourselves if we think that History, Literature and Religious Instruction are a major, or even a minor, source of moral values in the young. The prime source is the home.)

The prolonged, thorough and expert investigations of Peck and Havighurst are so important, and their educational implications so great, that the broad conclusions are worth quoting at some length. Summing up they say:

When each adolescent is considered by himself, his personality and character are linked with the nature of his family experience in an almost inexorably logical way. With only one possible exception in the whole research population, each adolescent is just about the kind of person that would be predicted from a knowledge of the way his parents treated him. Indeed, it seems reasonable to say that, to an almost startling degree, each child learns to feel and act, psychologically and morally, as just the kind of person his father and mother have been in their relationship with him.

This is not to say that other influences can in no circumstances be effective, but such influences 'seldom are intensively enough and personally enough exerted, in the typical American community, to make any noteworthy change in the character of its children, for good or ill'.

The same is almost certainly true of England. The danger is not that parents are of negligible influence on their children, but that no other influence can compete in effectiveness. Even 'socially mobile' children do not seem to develop values deeply at odds with their parents, at least while they are at school, although they may change their more outward habits of speech and deportment. Peck and Havighurst found no evidence of socially mobile children's conflict with parental values. The English grammar school has often been accused of, or praised for, instilling alien values into working-class children. This is a delusion as to the grammar school's potency. Working-class children in English grammar schools have not been shown to hold socio-moral values at odds with the working-class world.[20]

If schools are to make a real impact on the values, attitudes and behaviour of their pupils, they have probably got to be more aggressive and certainly more imaginative. They must organize themselves to provide personal experiences of a more profoundly intensive character than is commonly the case today, at least in our day schools.

The omnipotence of parents is buttressed rather than diminished by many social trends in the West today (and not least by the reduction in family size. As Bernard Shaw observed in his preface to *Misalliance* (1910): 'Two adult parents, in spite of a home to keep and an income to earn, can still interfere to a disastrous extent with the rights and liberties of one child.') The problem is not to restore parental influence, but to limit it. In particular, more protracted formal education and at the same time earlier marriage give parents not only influence but power into their children's adult years.

The author has argued elsewhere (in *Youth and the Social Order*, 1964) that early marriage is a sign of the power and economic independence of the young. Historically this is certainly true; and in England it is probably substantially true today. But there are clear signs in America that the middle-class young are marrying earlier whether they have achieved economic independence or not. In Britain young graduates are not yet so numerous and superabundant that they are chronically underpaid (and if they are still students they may have independent grants). In America they may be heavily dependent on their parents as they establish a home and meet the expenses of their first babies.

In her more recent writings (the 1962 Pelican edition of her *Male and Female*) Margaret Mead has emphasized this new dependence on parents which is consequent on early marriage, and recognizes that 'the breach between adolescent children and parents, so characteristic of American middle-class culture a generation ago, has narrowed . . .'. Sociologists have documented the large measure of dependence of young marrieds on their parents. Among middle-class families in New Haven in 1950 the involvement between the two generations was considerable, but the aid was all in one direction, from middle-aged parents to young married children. And the aid was substantial (though never in the form of regular allowances). It was provided for the purchase of a house and furniture, to meet the expenses of pregnancy and confinement. 'Affectional and economic ties still link the generational families and give stability to their relationships.'[21]

This is one of the politer ways of putting it. In fact young married adults are tied by a burden of indebtedness to their parents, even if there is no question of actually paying off the debt. This is part of a trend towards enhanced parental power. More protracted education and training in England as well as America are increasing the dependence of the young at working-class as well as at middle-class levels of society. As the legal and conventional ages of school leaving rise, and as underpaid apprenticeships multiply, the power of parents increases. The extension of education which in theory should emancipate the young, in fact guarantees their subservience.

SUBVERSIVE WIVES

The family is cohesive, its bonds are strong, its influence supreme. If it is at all in danger, it is less from the children than from their mothers. Women in the West have used their emancipation to weaken the family. This is perhaps not unreasonable. They have used their freedom to reduce the pressures and constraints to which the family bonds have traditionally subjected them.

As wives could seek divorce on the same grounds as men, since 1923, most petitions for divorce have been filed by wives (except during the years of the Second World War). In 1920 only 28·7 per cent of petitions were filed by women; in 1924, immediately after the passing of the Matrimonial Causes Act, the proportion was 61·1 per cent. Women were responsible for more than 50 per cent of the petitions in each of the inter-war years, and again in the years since 1947. No doubt they suffer more provocation to divorce than men; but they also had more to lose by it, particularly in the past when alternative employment, particularly for middle-class women, was difficult to obtain.

No social change is more dramatic than the rise of wives to power over the past century. Their legal disabilities have been removed; they are no longer endlessly pregnant and alternately producing and burying their young; and most important of all there are jobs for them to do at all social levels.

There are perhaps two principal sources of power for wives: on the one hand, tight-knit relationships with brothers and sisters and residence after marriage among her own folk ('uxori-local marriage'), so ensuring that the bride is flanked by her own kin; and on the other, independent earnings. In any society where one or both of these conditions prevail women are in a strong position *vis-à-vis* their husbands. It is perhaps no coincidence that in these societies marriage is relatively unstable. When husbands are in a position of dominance, marriage is secure.

The earnings of wives appeared to many nineteenth-century philanthropists as a threat to the family. When they legislated to protect working wives it was really to protect their husbands. Their intention was to reduce the wife's scope for industrial employment and domestic independence. In the debates on the Ten Hours Bill (1847) Lord Ashley objected to the factory employment of women because thereby they were 'gradually acquiring all those privileges which are held to be the proper portion of the male sex'. The stability of the family was thus endangered.

Karl Marx saw the employment of wives outside the home as leading to the 'breakup of the old family system within the organism of capitalist society', but thought more humane relationships for wives and children would result.[22] It is too obvious a point to need labouring, that when wives have independent earnings outside the home they have power within it. A young woman teacher today is worth thirty to forty thousand pounds (gross) to any man, even with breaks in her career for occasional child-bearing. Therein lies her assurance of domestic power. In his monumental study, *The Mothers* (1927), Briffault concluded from his broad survey of the family in history: 'Generally speaking, it is in those societies where they (women) toil most that their status is most independent. Where they are idle, they are as a rule little more than sexual slaves.' If wives today are more subversive than ever before, it is principally because one in three goes out to work, and the other two are often in a position to threaten to do so.

There seems to be an inverse correlation between the power of wives and the stability of marriage. In the 'mother-right' societies which have been studied by anthropologists the bonds of marriage are relatively light; in the 'father-right' societies they are commonly inflexible. ('Mother-right' refers essentially to the rights of the mother and her kin over her children; these are often reinforced by residence with the wife's people. This should not be confused with 'matriliny', which refers to inheritance through the female line, or with 'matriarchy', which refers to political rule by women. A matrilineal society is not necessarily a mother-right society, but will tend to be one.)

In the mother-right society the loyalty of brothers and sisters to one another is the supreme virtue and obligation. Sisters will never be co-wives of the same man, since their jealousies would endanger their solidarity. A wife will align herself with her sisters and her brothers if a disagreement arises with her husband; and he in turn will feel his strongest loyalty to his own sisters rather than his wife. But in the father-right societies children are 'children of their fathers'. (See for instance Margaret Read's study of the Ngoni, *Children of Their Fathers*.) Sororal polygyny may be common, for there is no objection to putting sisters under stress in the interests of marriage.

The Hausa of Nigeria, the Bemba of Rhodesia, the Ashanti of Ghana and the Lozi of Barotseland are all mother-right societies and in all marriage is unstable and divorce is common. The Baganda, the Azande (in the past), the Ngoni and the Zulus are father-right societies. Marriage is stable and divorce is rare. In the past the Zulus punished adultery with flogging or death. The stability or instability of marriage does not seem to be directly related to the size of the bride-price (the Azande of the Sudan had little divorce in the past, but marriage payments were small). The crucial circumstance seems to be the power of wives.

While it would no doubt be unwise to make too much of this, it does seem that wives behave as if they got less out of marriage than men. Durkheim used nineteenth-century suicide data to show that, while married men and women in general commit suicide less often than unmarried, when divorce is difficult or impossible, married women lose this superiority over spinsters, and when it is easy married men lose their superiority over bachelors. Men do not thrive on unstable marriage, women apparently do. In *Le Suicide* Durkheim propounds the law: 'Le mariage favorise d'autant plus la femme au point de vue du suicide que le divorce est plus pratiqué, et inversement.' In Italy, with very low divorce rates, married women were more prone to suicide than unmarried; in Prussia and Saxony, where divorce was common, married men were more prone to suicide than unmarried. 'Plus le lien conjugal se rompt souvent et facilement, plus la femme est favorisée par rapport à son mari.'

The advanced societies of the West have been remarkable this century for the power that wives have achieved and for the greater ease and frequency with which divorce is obtained. These circumstances are perhaps causally related. It is the men who require most a dependable domesticity, do most to promote it, and suffer most from its loss.

IV

A Threat to Society

SO SUCCESSFUL is the modern conjugal or nuclear family that it is a threat to society. It has lost its historic sociability. It is no longer a link between diverse social groups. It has imprisoned the father, a traditional liaison officer with the wider society outside the family, and it has imprisoned the children, even using the school as an extension of itself (particularly at the middle-class social level) rather than as a bridge to a wider and diversified social order.

THE UNSOCIABLE FAMILY

It seems that somewhere around the seventeenth century the West-European family turned its back on society. This happened first among the middle classes; today it is apparent at lower social levels. The sharp distinction between the public and the private is of comparatively recent date. (One symptom of this distinction was the conversion of public schools into exclusive private schools, although they retained their old and increasingly misleading name.)

In medieval and in Renaissance Europe a man's home was often his place of work or business and of entertainment. (At more affluent social levels it had its minstrels' gallery; more lowly homes were visited by players and jesters.) It was a public place and not a retreat from public affairs. Only the modern G.P. and parson, small shopkeeper and farmer retain a vestige of this earlier condition. Education was commonly centred on the household, whether the chivalric education of the great baronial home or the training of apprentices. (It was not only or even mainly the householder's children who assembled to be taught.) In medieval England the most important public affairs were conducted in a 'private' establishment, the household of the king. As Tout has observed: 'Absolutely no distinction existed between the sovereign in his private capacity as owner of a great estate and master of an extensive domestic establishment, and the sovereign in his public capacity as the political ruler of the nation.' Public officers were his private servants; the heart of government was to be found in the Chamber and the Wardrobe.

The sheer volume of pre-seventeenth-century domestic sociability is exhausting for the mid-twentieth-century suburbanite even to contemplate. The private household was an apron stage projecting into the tumult of public life; it was bursting with apprentices and servants; it was bombarded and invaded by the outside world. The great French scholar, Philippe Ariès, has described the seventeenth-century family as 'ouverte au monde, envahissant des amis, clients, serviteurs . . .'. The modern family, in contrast, consists of 'ce groupe de parents et d'enfants, heureux de leur solitude, étrangers au reste de la société . . .'.[1]

The modern family has not been eroded by 'individualism' or overwhelmed by society. 'Ce n'est pas l'individualisme qui a gagné, c'est la famille.' The elevation of the family in contradistinction and even direct opposition to wider society and its institutions (including schools) is clear and explicit in the writings of eighteenth-century and early-nineteenth-century social theorists. Society outside the family was a source of vice and contamination; only the family embodied and preserved the higher virtues. The child should be preserved from this alien and hostile outer world for as long as possible, even till manhood.

Perhaps the most powerful exponent of this view was the misanthropic Rousseau. For him all social institutions except the family were suspect. (At times, even the family: 'Man's weaknesses make him sociable. . . . A really happy man is a hermit.') All human institutions were tainted: 'Men are not made to be crowded together in ant-hills, but scattered over the earth to till it. The more they are massed together, the more corrupt they become' (*Émile*, Bk. I). A century earlier John Locke had looked on society as essentially beneficent, the great educator; and although he had championed domestic education, this was because the family was involved in society.

Rousseau approved of domestic education for the contrary reason, because it was the means of keeping the boy out of the world. For him the human group was naturally corrupt, whether the group of schoolboys or city dwellers. 'Of all creatures man is least fitted to live in herds.' Some contemporary theorists, though also sympathetic to the family and similarly hostile to other human associations, felt that Rousseau had gone too far. 'Rousseau . . . separates Emile from the world, as from a contagious region,' said David Williams in his *Lectures on Education*; 'attaches him to his governor; draws round them an enchanted circle; and sends them, involved as the planets of Des Cartes, in a vortex, to perform their evolutions in the world.'

In the early nineteenth century William Cobbett likewise showed a deep distrust of all social units other than the family. They could only be sources of depravity: the child should be encircled by his kin. But if, after all, the boy must be taken from his kin and sent to school, 'let it, if in your power, be as little populous as possible. . . . Jails, barracks, factories, do not corrupt by their walls, but by their condensed numbers. Populous cities corrupt for the same cause; and it is, because it must be, the same with schools, out of which children come not what they were when they went in.' (*Advice to Young Men.*)

The same sentiment is expressed perhaps still more forcefully by Thomas Guthrie in the middle of the nineteenth century. Social life outside the family was morally dangerous, for 'God never made men to be reared in flocks, but in families. Man is not a gregarious animal, other than that he herds together with his race in towns, a congeries of families. Born, as he is, with domestic affections, whatever interferes with their free play is an evil to be shunned, and, in its moral and physical results, to be dreaded.'[2] Ideally the home should be a self-sufficient social unit.

The new domestic ideal condemned many young people of middle- and upper-class families to incredible loneliness until their adult years. Ruskin, John Stuart Mill and Bertrand Russell, for example, had remarkably lonely lives in youth, with virtually no contact with others of their own age beyond the family circle. This withdrawn domesticity was recommended to parents in a spate of child-care books in the late eighteenth and early nineteenth centuries. (Mrs Sherwood's *Fairchild Family* is perhaps the best known; but there were many others, for example E. W. Benson's *Education at Home* published in 1824.)

Many people of independent means acted on this advice. Thus the grandfather of the late-Victorian poet and critic, Edmund Gosse, took his family to the wilds of Snowdonia so that no outside social influence should intrude on domestic self-sufficiency and he could conduct his children's education himself.

This was a far cry from the old tradition of domestic education represented by apprenticeship—education and training in *other people's* families, often of a different social level and perhaps in a different part of the country from one's own. In its heyday in the sixteenth and seventeenth centuries apprenticeship must have been one of the most powerful institutions binding society together. Sons of the gentry were apprenticed to trades and professions. Apprenticeship was the normal entry into such professions as engineering, pharmacy and medicine until Victorian days. It is a mistake to think of apprenticeship as the education and training only of artisans; like the public schools of the day—and the universities—it often brought together under the same roof the highest and the lowest in the land.

The duties of the master are clearly stated in 1662 by the Hallamshire cutlers. He should keep his apprentices 'under his rule, government, instruction and correction within his own house and among his own family where he dwells'. But by the early eighteenth century there are clear indications that the bourgeois family was resenting the intrusion of its privacy by other people's children. Masters were ever less inclined to take in apprentices and instruct them in a way of life as well as the technique of their craft.

Increasingly apprentices lived out. They paid premiums and claimed an independence which masters were in general only too pleased to concede. Defoe attacked these tendencies in his *Family Instructor*. From this time on the family felt and recognized an obligation only to its own children; although the Poor Law authorities tried to perpetuate the ideal of training and education by other people's families—through the system of 'parish apprenticeship'—until the middle of the nineteenth century.

In its extreme form the new ideal of self-contained domesticity was impossible of realization. Non-kinship institutions—social clubs, churches, schools—existed and flourished. And knowledge was increasingly public, best disseminated by public institutions. Families thrived as educational institutions when knowledge was ·private property, a mystery to be guarded against outsiders—and competitors.

All thoughtful contemporaries of Rousseau, Cobbett and Guthrie did not share their convictions. Indeed, ten years after Rousseau's *Émile* Helvétius published his famous *Traité de l'Homme*, in which he argued that between 8 and 18 the young should be removed almost continuously from their homes and parental influence. Nevertheless, Rousseau, Cobbett, Benson and Mrs Sherwood stand for a powerful current of thought which can be traced back into the eighteenth century: if the family could not in practice entirely displace other social institutions, it could at least provide a refuge from them.

The 'home-centred society' was not unheralded in mid-twentieth-century Britain. It is not simply a by-product of TV. But modern technics have aided a long established social trend. The motor car is a detachable parlour which enables the family to move off to the moors, the city or the coast still effectively insulated from all outside human contact. Contemporary migration to new housing developments has helped to pull even working-class fathers from their mates into exclusively domestic pursuits. 'La famille moderne,' observes Ariès, 'se retranche du monde et oppose à la société le groupe solitaire des parents et des enfants.' A movement pioneered by the middle classes, the retreat is now apparent at all levels of society.

Many sociologists have demonstrated how life in old-established working-class areas is neighbourhood-centred rather than family-centred: in Bethnal Green,[3] St Ebbe's in Oxford,[4] and traditional mining towns in the West Riding of Yorkshire.[5] Life turns outwards: the children towards the street play group, the wives towards their local kinsfolk, husbands towards their 'mates'. The men are deeply embedded in non-kinship groups. In the Yorkshire mining town 'A man's centre of gravity is outside his home; it is outside the home that there are located the criteria of success and social acceptance. He works and plays and makes contact with other men and women outside his home. The comedian who defined "home" as "the place where you fill the pools in on a Wednesday night" was something of a sociologist.'

But among the younger wives, even in Yorkshire, many now see their husbands more often than in bed. And in areas where young couples have moved from old-established districts to new estates, husband and wife have been forced into closer proximity and even co-operation through sheer loneliness. Willmott and Young have observed of new estates near London: 'Husband and wife are together and a closer partnership here can make isolation bearable.' (*Family and Kinship in East London.*) 'The newcomers are surrounded by strangers instead of kin. Their lives outside the family are no longer centred on people; their lives are centred on the house. This change from a people-centred to a house-centred existence is one of the fundamental changes resulting from migration.'

Husband and wife turn in upon themselves and upon their younger children. The husband does many jobs around the home previously considered the special province of women. He even baths the baby—quite often if he is a white-collar worker, but by no means infrequently, today, if he is a labourer. John and Elizabeth Newson found in their recent inquiries in Nottingham (reported in their *Infant Care in an Urban Community*, 1963) that 52 per cent of fathers were 'highly participant' in looking after the baby, and 27 per cent 'moderately participant'. Shop and office workers were particularly participant (61 per cent highly); 36 per cent of labourers were highly participant.

The Newsons refer to 'this massive change in the masculine role' which, they conclude, has occurred principally over the past thirty years. Father's place today is firmly in the home. 'The willingness of so many fathers to participate actively in looking after such young children is, we believe, a very distinctive feature of modern family life in England.'

Similar trends have been described in America. They have been deplored at least by Margaret Mead.

> The care of very young infants by their fathers is something that no former civilization has encouraged among their educated and responsible men. Delight in motherhood has been recognized as a principal barrier to women's creativeness in work, but there is now added the danger that delight in parenthood may prove equally seductive to young men. (*Male and Female*.)

The home-centred society which we have evolved is a serious threat to social cohesion. Intensive family relationships are developed at the expense of wider social contacts. Margaret Mead refers to 'This turning in upon the home for all satisfaction, with a decrease in friendship, in community responsibility, in work and creativeness . . .'. Ariès has offered similar reflections on the contemporary scene. 'On est tenter de penser,' he writes, 'que le sentiment de la famille et la sociabilité n'étaient pas compatibles, et ne pouvaient se développer qu'aux depens l'un de l'autre.'

The English family is increasingly an isolated and emotionally self-sufficient social atom. When Geoffrey Gorer conducted an inquiry into English social life in 1951, he found that a quarter of his national sample gave no answer when asked what social groups and associations they belonged to outside the family and immediate neighbourhood. Young married people, especially wives living in large towns on small incomes, were the loneliest members of English society. Twenty-five per cent of this sample preferred the company of their immediate family to all other (but unmarried daughters at higher social levels tended to be confined to their family circle although they would have preferred to be elsewhere). Men as compared with women preferred family activities to all other in the ratio of four to three.[6]

The professionalization of local services (defence, taxation, law enforcement, road development and so on) which has proceeded apace over the past two centuries has left the individual citizen with nothing of much importance that he must do outside the home. For all practical purposes citizenship today can be defined in terms of purely domestic obligations. Added to this is the seductive comfort of the modern home. Public places—even the refurbished public house—cannot compete with it in splendour. 'The new man,' says Mark Abrams, 'stays at home, and he is likely to find burdensome and repugnant any activities or interests that force him to leave the family circle and to forgo part of his domestic privacy and comfort.' 'If his outside contacts are weakened and reduced in favour of his home ties, this will affect all his group relations. Reduced attendance at trades-union meetings, at Friendly Societies and other club activities, at political discussions, and at all forms of outdoor mass entertainment and activity will inevitably affect his attitudes towards the social institutions they serve.'[7] We can expect that for some time to come the need to engage in regular work will interrupt his care of the baby; and while we retain our present rules of incest, he must still, if unmarried, go forth to find a mate.

AN ECCENTRIC INSTITUTION

The Zulus say: 'We marry our enemies.' This is an excellent prescription for any society, a sound principle of social cohesion which today is in danger of neglect. To a disastrous extent we nowadays marry our friends. If the kinship system fails to unite potential enemies, then other social institutions—perhaps the school system—must.

Our modern system of romantic marriage in the West is a curious aberration of comparatively recent time, an eccentric condition of the 'advanced' societies. Marriage in our own society in the past, and in many social systems throughout the world today, has had a more difficult job than the provision of companionship, stable sexual satisfaction, and the support of young children; it has been a principal mechanism of social cohesion, of uniting conflicting social interests and groups.

Today in England and America the two sets of grandparents are even expected to be friends. Margaret Mead has commented on this American trend for marriage 'within narrower limits of class and religious groupings, and instead of the former expectation of incompatibility among the two sets of grandparents, co-grandparents today expect to be congenial allies in supporting their dependent married children'.

This abnormal condition is relatively new. In European history the contrary function of marriage in harnessing enemies can be seen most clearly among aristocratic and royal houses. Rival and dangerous nations and dynasties have traditionally provided wives and husbands for members of the royal family. When friendship has not after all been maintained with France, Spain or Germany, and we have found ourselves at war, we have been in the embarrassing position of numbering the uncles and cousins of royalty among our foes.

When we take a broad view of human marriage through time and space, we see that it is typically and normally a diplomatic arrangement, always in some sense a 'marriage of state'. Its essential purpose is to establish an alliance between different and often opposed social groups. The two individuals who are immediately concerned are an irrelevance. From his broad survey of human marriage Robert Briffault concluded that 'Marriage, then, is almost universally regarded not as a contract between a man and a woman but between the groups to which they belong. No feature is more marked and more general. . . .'

This is the perspective of the anthropologist. Modern Western marriage appears parochial after examining marriage systems throughout the world. In introducing an impressive survey of African marriage Radcliffe-Brown comments:

> the modern English idea of marriage is recent and decidedly unusual, the product of a particular social development. We think of marriage as an event that concerns primarily the man and woman who are forming a union and the State, which gives that union its legality and alone can dissolve it by divorce. The consent of parents is, strictly, only required for minors. [8]

Seen in the perspectives of history and anthropology our system is socially irresponsible.

Marriage involves the loss of a member by one social group, which 'gives away' that member. Marriage is the social equivalent of murder, for which due compensation must be made, restoring the balance and equilibrium of society. In Anglo-Saxon times the groom gave a symbolic payment, the 'wed', to the bride's kinsmen. (He gave a more substantial payment to the bride's father.) This survives in the wedding ring, a present not to the bride's kinsfolk but to the bride herself—a highly significant change.

This restitution or compensation takes many different forms in different societies. Under the system of 'exchange-marriage' formerly practised by the Tiv of Nigeria, the groom gave a sister in return for his bride. More commonly a bride-price is paid which not only compensates the bride's kin for the loss of her services, but helps to guarantee the marriage, since it is returnable if the marriage breaks up.

There is considerable dispute among anthropologists about the precise significance of the bride-price (or 'bride-wealth', as many prefer) in African marriage. Evans-Pritchard has argued that it is not in fact 'economic blackmail' designed to ensure the stability of marriage. Gluckman sees a connection between marriage stability and bride-wealth, but inverts the usual relationship: stability is not promoted by a large payment, but a large payment is possible if marriage is stable. But whatever the precise arrangements and their consequences, the implication is that marriage concerns social groups, at once tending to upset the balance between them and yet promoting their alliance. Marriage counsellors of modern Britain are a poor substitute for a phalanx of truly involved kinsfolk. What is so remarkable about any contemporary Western marriage is that it should as a rule be so stable when so few people of consequence have a stake in its existence.

Marriage into a different or even hostile social group promotes a community of interests, perhaps in the property arrangements and mergers which accompany and ratify it, and certainly in the grandchildren. All marriages are in some sense mixed, although extreme and unapproved mixtures may promote more conflict than amity.

The grandchildren may be a more important link between the social groups than either spouse. In many non-literate societies the father is not really 'one of the family' (he was scarcely one of the family in Bethnal Green). He has little importance in the household of his wife and their children; he is little more than a visitor for stud purposes, although in spite of this—or perhaps because of it—he may be quite kindly regarded. His wife turns to her brother for support and guidance for her children. (Her husband is similarly a man of consequence and authority in *his* sister's household.) Among the Ashanti of West Africa the husband is of little consequence in his family-by-marriage. He has a stronger social link with his sisters than his wife, with whom he probably does not live. The children of the Lozi of Barotseland are important to both sides of the family; they make their home in the village of either their mother's or their father's kin and inherit there. But their father has only a tenuous connection with his in-laws and even with his wife. He confides in and feels loyalty towards his sister rather than his wife.

It would be unwise to put forward mixed marriage as a universal cure for all our social divisions and disunities. Only when it really involves both groups of kin, and both are prepared to accept the marriage, however grudgingly, can it establish a link between them. But when social classes, religious and ethnic groups—or even occupational groups —marry exclusively among their own kind, social disunity and division are likely unless other effective forms of inter-relationship are established.

Unions between people of different colour have not produced a unified society in Jamaica, although Lord Olivier, writing in 1907 (*White Capital and Coloured Labour*), was confident that they would. When to differences of colour are added differences of social class, the gulf is difficult to bridge. Mixed marriages can often surmount one barrier (colour or class or religion) but seldom two or three (colour and class and perhaps religion). West Indians and West Africans who have married girls in England, usually at their own social level, have often been successfully absorbed into the white community. (Asiatics, on the other hand, have usually tried to absorb their white wives into their own communities and to bring up their children in their own culture.) When marriages with West Indians and West Africans have failed to have this effect, it has often been because the girls were *already* abandoned by their families.[9]

There is little doubt that we are today a deeply divided society. Marriage is to a high degree 'assortative', between people of the same kind; and we have no other effective social institutions bridging the gap between the disparate social groups.

It seems probable that the educational ladder which we have erected in this century has had the effect of diminishing the proportion of marriages occurring across social class lines. Ambitious young men of lowly social origin need no longer marry 'above themselves' in order to get on in life. It is probably easier and less exhausting to pass examinations than to lay siege to the boss's daughter. Education has displaced marriage as a major means of social ascent (but it may provide us with top people with less initiative and resourcefulness in personal relationships). At the same time 'superfluous' daughters of the middle class (estimated at 30 per cent in Victorian England) need no longer marry beneath themselves: with the dramatic expansion of suitable employment for them in the course of this century, if they cannot find husbands of suitable social rank, they can become or remain teachers, nurses, doctors, secretaries.

In her distinguished study of steel and hosiery manufacturers over the past century Charlotte Erickson found that men who rose from relatively humble origins to top positions did so more often through marriage than through education. ' "Good" marriages accompanied the rise of men from Social Classes II, III and IV to prominence more frequently than "good" education. It was perhaps easier for an ambitious young man to marry above his station than to be educated above his station even in the early twentieth century.'[10]

The considerable degree of assortative mating which exists among marriages contracted in the years since 1940 is no less than among marriages contracted in 1915. An inquiry in 1949 with a national sample of some six thousand marriages showed no significant tendency for marriage to occur more frequently today between people of different social origin. Those most likely to marry outside their 'social class' were children of skilled manual workers; those least likely to do so were the children of professional and managerial parents on the one hand, and of unskilled labourers on the other.[11]

In the sample as a whole 45 per cent of the married couples came from families of the same social level. In 71 per cent of the marriages husband and wife had received a similar type of education; and 83 per cent had either similar social origins or similar education. (Approximately 30 per cent of the men in the sample had 'married down', only a quarter of the women; but fewer women than men in the sample had upper-class origins, and more men must in consequence marry down if they were to marry at all.) Four social grades were distinguished in the inquiry. Only 11·3 per cent of wives and of husbands had married two or three grades above or below their rank of origin.

Between 1915 and 1940 there had been a stronger tendency for men and women of different educational standards to marry, but the trend for like to marry like was pronounced at both dates. There was a particularly strong tendency for university graduates to marry university graduates.

If graduates marry graduates, teachers teachers, doctors doctors, clerks clerks, factory workers factory workers, the cross-linkings and interconnections of our social system are impoverished. And other social institutions are failing precisely where marriage is failing. The evidence is overwhelming that people of different levels of occupation and education are not coming together to any significant extent in residential neighbourhoods, clubs, pubs, churches, or any other form of social organization.

In Worcester, Banbury and Glossop the same divisions have been recorded, the failure of people of different occupational and educational levels to meet and engage together in common pursuits. It is not primarily wealth but outlook and interests which keep them apart. 'George Bourne', writing his *Change in the Village* before the First World War, thought that this cleavage was something new in twentieth-century England and attributed it chiefly to education: 'It is a question of civilization far more than wealth that divides the employing classes from the employed. . . . In beliefs and tastes they (the employing classes) are a new kind of people. They have new kinds of knowledge.' A social mechanism which has in the past—in the shape of pre-Victorian apprenticeship, public schools and universities—forged links between different social groups increasingly holds them apart.

A TASK FOR EDUCATION

Schools were generally trusted and extensively used by the middle classes when they became an extension of the middle-class home. This occurred in the third and fourth decades of the nineteenth century. The school now demonstrated that it could beat the family at its own (comparatively new) game —provide a protective and enclosed environment, with all the children of the same social background and religious faith. Henceforth the children whom a boy or girl encountered at school would be indistinguishable from those who might be invited to his birthday party at home.

Before this time, when a boy went off to his public school he received a truly public, and not a private or domestic, education. In the days before boarding houses were generally established, he was exposed to a wide range of social contacts not only in school but outside it. The boarding houses in a public school town were more like boarding houses at Blackpool—even when the landlady was the wife of a member of the school staff. Such boarding houses were, in many instances, only slowly incorporated into the schools and the house master's profits from his boarders thereby to some extent controlled). Boarding arrangements of the modern kind were surprisingly late at some schools—at Harrow, for instance, not until the eighteen-thirties.

In seventeenth- and eighteenth-century England the public school confronted the schoolboy with the public— children from very varied social backgrounds, and the life of the town, or at least of the family with whom he lodged. The boy who went to school went into life.

This was as true of France as of England, as Ariès has observed: 'les écoliers logeaient chez des bourgeois de la ville, libres de toute autorité, tant paternelle qu' académique: à peu près rien dans leur mode de vie ne les distinguait des adultes célibataires. Bientôt, maîtres et parents jugèrent cette liberté excessive. Une discipline autoritaire et hiérarchique s'établissait au collège. . . .'

This medieval tradition conflicted with the new bourgeois

ideal of protected domesticity. The new schools of Victorian England—the refashioned public schools, the endowed grammar schools seeking to enhance their status, and the new proprietary schools, to say nothing of the plague of genteel private academies—offered the protected environment of the ideal home: fellow pupils of the same social rank, the same social and moral values, the same religious beliefs. This was the condition of their success. The Quaker parent need no longer keep his child isolated at home: he could with confidence entrust his son to Bootham (1823), for instance, or to Leighton Park (1899); the Methodist to Woodhouse Grove (1812) or the Leys School (1874); the Catholic to the Oratory School (1859) or Beaumont (1861); the Primitive Methodist to Elmfield College (1864); the Anglican to a school in the appropriate social division of the Woodard Foundation. School and home were now continuous.

Before Victoria's reign the ancient endowed schools were protected against parents by the law. This was the point of the founder's charter, scrupulously upheld by the courts, which defined the curriculum and often the social recruitment of the school. In the second quarter of the nineteenth century private schools multiplied, offering the curriculum and social contacts of which parents approved. Many ancient foundations found astute and ruthless headmasters (like Arnold at Rugby, Vaughan at Harrow and Kennedy at Shrewsbury) who were able to circumvent the intentions of the founder with regard both to the curriculum and the type of boy admitted.

The eighteen-twenties and thirties saw a rapid expansion of private school education. The Taunton Commission found in 1864 that there were more boys in private than endowed schools and was dismayed by the pressures which parents were able to bring to bear upon the staff. Mr Fitch reported from Yorkshire that in the bigger private schools it seemed that 'each parent had made a separate contract as to the amount of comfort and attention his child should receive'.

A Task for Education

The most explicit statement of the view that schools were only tolerable when they were an extension of the home is to be found in the late nineteenth-century writings of Charlotte Mason, notably in the many editions of her books, *Parents and Children* and *Home Education*. She spoke of the times in family life when relations were strained, 'and of these, the moment when the child feels himself consciously a member of the school republic is one of the most trying. Now, all the tact of the parents is called into play. Now, more than ever, it is necessary that the child should be aware of the home authority, just that he knows how he stands, and how much he is free to give the school.'

Home and school should merge, with the home as senior partner. Parents should 'keep up with their children, should know where they are and how they are getting on in their studies, should look into their books, give an eye to their written work, be ready with an opinion, a hint, a word of encouragement'. Although this was useful to pupil and teacher, 'of more consequence is it that the parents themselves keep their place as heads of the family'.

The purpose of schools is the pursuit of truth, and many find offensive or even improper the discussion of education as a piece of social machinery. But education is a social institution with profound social effects quite apart from the intellectual and moral truths it may propound. It can divide society, or it can help to unite it.

Schools which are extensions of families narrow the child's social range. They stunt his intellectual development and blunt his moral awareness and sympathies. They keep him from contact with adults except teachers and kinsmen; they prolong his immaturity. ('La famille et l'école,' observes Ariès, 'ont ensemble retiré l'enfant de la société des adultes.') If schools are to become our principal means of social integration—even our principal means of education —they must regain their truly public character.

V

The 'Good Home'

THE 'GOOD HOME' is an aid to success in our school system. It is small; the parents are ambitious for their children; the father is at least a skilled manual worker; and if it is a working-class home, the mother has preferably 'married down'. The father is somewhat ineffectual, perhaps rather feckless; but one or both parents are demanding, even ruthless in their expectations of achievement. Relationships in the home are emotionally bleak. The family is unstable and has moved often; the mother goes to work. The children grow up to be rather withdrawn and solitary, conscientious and given to self-blame. They are 'good grammar-school material'.

BIRTH-ORDER AND FAMILY SIZE

The feature of the 'good home' which is least in doubt is its size. In general the small family produces the most intelligent children as measured by intelligence tests, presumably because 'intelligence' is to a considerable extent inherited, and intelligent parents show their intelligence by limiting the size of their families.

It is also possible that in the small family the child is in closer touch with its parents and habitually uses more grown-up language and ideas than he would if he were lost in a cloud of siblings. He may therefore appear to have a higher level intelligence than he 'really' has, particularly on tests which are wholly or mainly verbal. The trend to smaller families may thus, conceivably, mask a real decline in innate intelligence by giving a boost to the environmental component.

72

The negative correlation of approximately point three between intelligence and family size has been established in numerous surveys, such as the Scottish Mental Survey of 1947. A correlation of this magnitude means, roughly, that in a random sample of a hundred families, sixty would demonstrate this relationship; but in twenty there would be high average intelligence in large families, and in the remaining twenty low average intelligence in small families.

If intelligent parents are not directed by their intelligence to limit their families, then their families may be large and their children of high intelligence. There does not appear to be the same connection between family size and intelligence among Catholic as among Protestant families (and presumably in the past, before the advent of modern birth-control methods, there was no connection in the population at large). In one fairly recent survey in Middlesbrough only 6 per cent of children from families of four or more children gained grammar school places, but 18 per cent of Catholic children from families of this size did so. Catholic children from small families showed no such superiority.[1]

It seems that even children of good intelligence will not use their intelligence as effectively as they might if they are members of large families, particularly when their fathers are manual workers. In her inquiries in boys' grammar schools in 1951 Himmelweit found that working-class boys from small families (one or two children) had a better chance of gaining a grammar school place than working-class boys from large families. 'Since no such differences were found in the non-manual groups they require an explanation over and above that of the known negative correlation between I.Q. and family size.'[1]

More recently, in his research on a national sample of primary school children, Douglas found that middle-class boys (but not girls) were also less likely to succeed in the eleven plus selection tests if they came from large families. However, in the middle class it was only families of four or more children that had a depressing effect; among working-class children the prospects became progressively worse as the family increased in size above one or two.[3]

In working-class families of three children, 14·1 per cent were expected to gain grammar school places judging by their measured abilities, but only 13·2 per cent did so; in middle-class families of the same size 33·9 per cent were expected to gain places, and a still higher percentage (38·6) in fact did so. The explanation appears to lie very largely in the attitudes, expectations and assumptions of parents with large families. If the school is very good, and if the parents' attitudes are favourable, the handicap for working-class children from large families can almost, though not entirely, be eliminated.

The significance of birth-order is also reasonably well established, although the interpretation of the facts is neither easy nor certain. In his nineteenth-century studies of eminent scientists Galton found that it was an advantage to be an eldest or an only son. Subsequent research in the general population both here and in America has amply confirmed this judgement.

Social-class differences have been found in this connection too. It matters much more to be an eldest son or daughter in a working-class than a middle-class family, at least as far as eleven plus selection is concerned. One investigation demonstrated that 'a working-class boy, whatever the size of his family, is more likely to attend a grammar school if he is an eldest child, and . . . this again does not apply in the case of a middle-class boy . . .'.[4]

Douglas's findings were similar. The eldest child tended, in the eleven plus examinations, to exceed the expectations based on his measured ability. This was found to be the case among both middle-class and working-class children, but to a more marked extent among the latter.

Douglas did not find that only children did any better than 'expected', and attributed this principally to lack of sibling rivalry. Other investigators have found both onlys and eldests more scholastically able than intermediates and youngests. There is no evidence that they are more intelligent; they are more disposed to use their intelligence with effect in the school setting.

Lees and Stewart established in two Midland cities in 1955 that both eldests and onlys were found in grammar schools significantly more often than in modern schools. Thus onlys were 18·3 per cent of the grammar school population in one city, but only 11·7 per cent of the modern school population. The advantage of being an eldest girl diminished in families of four or more.[5]

The interpretation of these findings is not easy. In earlier research into the background of a group of adult students Lees, like Douglas, attributed the superiority of eldests principally to sibling rivalry, particularly when younger brothers and sisters were getting on well and so seriously threatening the eldest's status.[6] Clearly this cannot account for the success of onlys; and in their later work Lees and Stewart advance an explanation which might apply to any first-born child—his rather lonely position of eminence and perhaps responsibility in the family which provides him with an early training for handling 'situations demanding individual initiative, and, incidentally, of coping with such situations as those presented by intelligence tests and examinations at eleven plus years'.

This explanation is diametrically opposed to that offered by Stanley Schachter to account for the superiority in some situations of first-born Americans. Lees and Stewart say the first-born is successful because he has a capacity for loneliness; Schachter says he is successful because he has not.

First-born children, argues Schachter, are less rather than more able to cope on their own with their problems and anxieties. Far from being highly 'individualistic', they will seek solutions to their problems in groups. First-borns undergoing group therapy have been observed to continue their treatment longer than necessary; later-borns drop out before they should. There is a greater tendency for later-borns to become alcoholics, handling their anxieties in non-social ways. The first-born, as an infant, has enjoyed a concerned and attentive mother, fussing over her first child:

she has come to his side whenever he faced discomfort or fear. Later-born children have a mother who is probably more blasé; they will more often be left to deal with their problems alone and will grow up accustomed to handling their anxieties in solitude.[7]

The significance of birth order has attracted a great deal of attention. Much has been written about it and psychologists have conducted a variety of experiments to check their theories. Recent experiments by Sampson in America indicate that first-born males, at least, are inclined to greater social conformity: they fall into line more readily when rewards are offered and are more susceptible to social pressures. (They also have a stronger need for achievement than later-borns.) First-born girls, on the other hand, showed a greater independence than later-borns.[8] It is not easy to reconcile these findings, particularly with regard to sex differences, with other research, although in a general sense they are in line with Schachter. But it seems reasonable to suggest that first-born boys at any rate may be successful in our school system not because they are individualistic, but because they are not: because they need the approval of adults and conform closely to the expectations of teachers.

'FAVOURABLE PARENTAL ATTITUDES'

The importance of parental attitudes to a child's progress at school seems to be firmly established. Yet the concept of 'favourable parental attitude' is perhaps one of the most ambiguous and misleading in the contemporary discussion of educational achievement. The measurement of this attitude has been crude in the extreme; and precisely what has been measured is open to very serious doubt. It would be very dangerous indeed to equate parental interest and concern with kindly, beneficent and understanding encouragement. The usual measures of parental interest might equally signify ruthless, unreasoning, inexorable and even quite unrealistic demands.

The most common and apparently objective measure of

parental interest is the frequency of visits to school. Middle-class parents score high here, and working-class mothers higher than working-class fathers. But while the frequency of school visits undoubtedly provides some indication of the level of parental interest, it also measures the level of parents' social competence and assurance.

Other factors which have usually been taken into account are the age at which parents wish their children's education to end; and the type of school or institution of further education they wish them to attend. (One inquiry, for example, obtained favourable–unfavourable attitude scores according to (1) the frequency of parents' school visits, (2) their preference for selective secondary education, (3) the intention to keep the child at school until at least 16, and (4) their preference for further education after school.[9]) The longer the period of education envisaged and the more selective and academic the type of institution preferred, the more favourable is parental attitude judged to be.

Attempts have been made to take into account more intangible aspects of parents' attitudes, but these are often difficult to incorporate into attitude scales. Teachers' judgements of parental interest have also been taken into account (by Douglas), and cultural interests have been estimated in the light of the Sunday newspapers they take, their membership of public libraries and cultural organizations. The emotional atmosphere of the home has been estimated, the degree of harmony prevailing, and the emotional security afforded the child. The level of material wellbeing in the home is easier to establish; and it has been shown (in Middlesbrough) that below a certain level, low material standards may nullify the advantages of favourable parental attitudes as conventionally judged by visits to the school and ambitions for the child.

There is no doubt that parents who visit the school often and wish their children to enjoy a selective and protracted education in general give a boost to their children's educational progress. At all social levels, and in socially contrasted areas, children tend to be more successful in the eleven plus examinations if they have parents who have discussed their future with the primary school teacher and would prefer them to stay at school till 18.[10] There are clear signs in recent research that parental interest (measured by similar crude means) is more important with children of borderline ability, and from working-class rather than middle-class homes.

This is the conclusion of Douglas's report on his national sample of primary school children. Children of borderline ability obtained 23 per cent more places in grammar schools than had been expected in the light of their measured ability, if their parents were educationally ambitious for them; but they gained 69 per cent fewer places if their parents were unambitious. Children with ambitious parents tended to be 'over-achievers'. When the school's academic standard, the material standards of the home, and parental ambitions were analysed for their relative importance, parental encouragement was shown to have the greatest effect.

'Parental encouragement' is not necessarily the same thing as humane consideration and kindly, understanding interest. It may be a ruthless and inflexible demand for achievement. When 'family dynamics' have been investigated by clinical psychologists for their bearing on achievement, unambitious parents have obviously been of little help to their children; but neither have 'normal' parents, setting reasonable and realistic goals. The most effective parents are, it is true, ambitious for their children; but it is not a particularly attractive characteristic, ruthless and demanding.

This is the picture that emerges from the research of Kent and Davis in Cambridgeshire, and is amply supported by inquiries in America. Kent and Davis investigated the relationship between 'discipline in the home' and intellectual development among a sample of primary school children (as well as a group of juvenile offenders and children referred to a psychiatric outpatients' clinic). The homes of the children were investigated and classified as 'normal', 'unconcerned', 'over-anxious' and 'demanding'.

'Normal' parents were tolerant, patient, but firm, making reasonable demands on the child, realistically related to his abilities, interests and needs. The unconcerned were indifferent to the child's progress, without ambition for his success, content if he kept out of trouble and made few demands upon them. But the effective home was the 'demanding' home: the parents set high standards from an early age; they were ambitious for their child; they 'reward infrequently and without generosity'; approval and affection are conditional upon achievement. But within the general framework of high demands and expectations the child is free to learn and good opportunities are afforded for him to do so. In the light of other research on achievement which is reviewed in the next section, it is perhaps the conjunction of demands and opportunity which is important.

Such homes were not confined to middle-class social levels. Whatever their social position, they tended more than other types of home to produce children of high ability. 'One may argue therefore that the cause of the high development of verbal and academic abilities lies in their demanding discipline, and that the poor development of these abilities in the children of the unconcerned class is due to the lack of encouragement given them by their parents.'[11]

There seem to be few rewards in our educational system (and perhaps in our society generally) for 'normality' or even for humanity. The driving, demanding home, with exacting standards and expectations and remorseless pressure on the children, appears to be the 'good home'. The kindly, reasonable, understanding, tolerant and helpful home pays less handsome dividends. This may be why frequent moves, working mothers, and wives who have married beneath themselves are valuable ingredients in the good home: they are symptoms or causes of the striving and straining which seems so invaluable.

Research in America into the family background of able schoolchildren and university students lends support to the view that family relationships which are demanding and lacking in warmth are associated with high intellectual capacity. In their studies of adolescents who were of high intelligence but comparatively low in 'creativity' on the one hand, and of others who were of rather lower intelligence but high in creativity on the other, Getzels and Jackson found that the former more often had mothers who were 'vigilant', 'critical' and 'less accepting'. Mothers of the children of high I.Q. both observed more about their children and observed a greater number of objectionable qualities. The mothers of the children who did best in tests of creativity apparently subjected their children to a less intensive and censorious scrutiny; and they were more at ease with themselves and with the world.[12] (We are given no information about fathers.)

American studies of university students are in general congruent with these findings. Very thorough investigations have been made of the academic performance, personality development, family background and subsequent careers of the women graduates of Vassar College. The early family life of 'under-achievers' at college had been happy and secure. 'Fathers are seen as having been competent, loving, lots of fun. . . . Mothers were warm, sociable, happy and accepting.' Over-achievers, on the other hand, tended to have mothers with high social aspirations and fathers who were self-made men. 'On the whole there is close conformity with strict parental demands.'

Those graduates who achieved distinction in their subsequent careers (typically by middle life they had not married or had few children if they had) did well in their studies at Vassar. They had been lonely at college and 'In their early life and adolescence they have experienced conflict arising from domineering and talented mothers, against whom there is considerable repressed hostility associated with strong guilt. As a group their early lives tended not to be free from upsetting events such as deaths, moves, economic crises and the like, nor were their childhoods outstandingly happy.'[13]

A more impressionistic picture is given by Jackson and Marsden, in their study of 'Marburton', of the home circumstances of successful grammar school pupils. Sixth-formers in 'Marburton' came mainly from driving and ambitious homes with frustrated parents who belonged to the 'sunken middle class' and fathers who were foremen without hope of rising to managerial rank. Some of the children, successful at the grammar school, in the end failed their degrees. For one girl this failure brought a great sense of release: 'I decided then and there that I'd go and do what I wanted. I'd been doing what other people wanted for so long and now it was time that I did what I wanted. I went to the employment exchange and they offered me all kinds of academic things—but I decided definitely that I was going nursing.'[14]

Kent and Davis found frequent moves of home closely related to the highly productive demanding discipline. 'An especially large proportion of the children of the "demanding" class had experienced three or more moves' compared with the normal class. Douglas found a similar situation: 'When the average test performance of children of families which have never moved is compared with the performance of those in families that have moved, it is found that the former make lower average scores in the tests than the latter. . . .' But there were slight indications that the disadvantages of a stable home-background were less marked for pre-school children.

Investigations in an American university have isolated early geographical mobility as a common factor in the background of students of high ability who, when subjected to a battery of personality and attitude tests, undervalued themselves, felt insecure and lonely, and were strongly-inclined towards guilt feelings and self-punishment. These able students had one significant early experience in common: geographical instability. 'In all of their histories are accounts of moving from one town to another. One of the girls probably expressed the feelings of the group when she wrote in her autobiography, "Several times I was dead sure that my whole life was being torn completely asunder. . . ."'[15]

Of course such a history of family instability is not a necessary condition of academic excellence. And it would be a mistake to ascribe the intellectual development associated with it to the stimulus of changing environments. The migrant home is often the striving home, and it is the attitudes of migrant parents rather than the migration itself which probably accounts for these findings. The value to working-class children of a mother who has 'married down'[16] perhaps has a similar explanation: she strives to make up for her social decline through the achievements of her children.

The fact that mothers go to work is also more commonly a symptom of parental striving and ambition than of selfishness and negligence, and for this reason assists rather than impedes the child's educational progress. During research in Aberdeen, Frazer found no evidence that children were handicapped at the secondary stage by having a mother at work: 'if there is any difference at all, it appears to be very slightly in favour of the children whose mothers go out to work, especially in the middle ranges of intelligence'.[17]

In America there is more positive evidence that working mothers may foster educational ambitions and promote higher attainment. The greater tendency for urban as opposed to rural wives to take up paid employment outside the home has been held to account for the backwardness of rural children. 'A mother who works at least part time in a small town or larger city is likely to be exposed to the fact that a college education is required for most high status jobs, whereas the mother who is submerged in the home-making problems of a farm family is unlikely to be impressed with this reality.'[18]

PERMISSION AND PUNISHMENT

One of the most interesting but as yet rather inconclusive ways of examining the influence of family background has been to compare social groups which differ significantly in their general level of occupational and educational achievement. Urban children are generally superior to rural children; middle-class children to working-class children; the children of Jewish immigrants to the United States to Italian immigrants. Can broad differences in attainment between these groups (of course there is a great deal of overlap too) find an explanation in differences in child-care practices and family dynamics?

The general tendency for middle-class children to do better in the school system in both England and America has been attributed not only to differences in parental encouragement but to social-class differences in early child rearing practices. The training of middle-class infants, it is argued, makes them particularly able to succeed later on in scholastic pursuits and perhaps in the activities involved in professional work. Working-class children of good intelligence may be defective in other attributes which ensure academic success. Whatever the long term consequences of social-class differences in infant care, there can be no doubt that these differences are still with us. As the Newsons observe after their recent exhaustive investigations in Nottingham: 'The classless society in Britain is still a long way off. Men may be born equal; but, within its first month in the world, the baby will be adapting to a climate of experience that varies according to its family's social class.'[19]

Scholastically able people are not only intelligent, they also tend to be conscientious, capable of long-term effort and planning, able to forgo many immediate satisfactions for more distant gains. Often, too, they are orderly, careful, meticulous, and punctual. Some or all of these attributes have been ascribed to the stricter methods of infant care which are perhaps characteristically middle-class: early and severe toilet training; early punishment of aggression; feeding by rigid schedule, and early weaning; early independence training; and control through 'love-oriented' techniques of discipline. It has also been claimed that middle-class upbringing induces 'adaptive, socialized anxiety' which deters the child from incurring the disapproval of his parents and teachers.[20] Working-class upbringing, though not unproductive of anxieties too, was supposed to be more permissive and indulgent, less likely to produce far-sighted, controlled and conscientious personalities.

These views are currently under heavy fire. The relevance of early toilet training to a controlled and orderly adult personality has been seriously questioned.[21] Hallworth has shown that the academically successful are not generally more anxious, at least at the secondary school stage, than the less academically gifted.[22] But most startling of all has been the apparent demonstration both in England and America that the middle classes are more permissive and less punitive in their child-care practices than the working classes. These claims need very careful scrutiny for the limits of their validity.

Recent research with mothers in Devonshire seemed to show that, with reference to 5-year-old children, 'In England, as in the U.S.A., middle-class mothers are less punitive than working-class mothers,' and that 'English middle-class mothers are also like American middle-class mothers in being more permissive of aggressive behaviour.'[23] And indeed there seems little doubt that with regard to 'immodesty' and aggression the middle-class mother of today is more permissive than twenty or thirty years ago. She has been lectured by the psychologists, and she has taken heed. This was clear too in the Newsons' study of mothers of one-year-old babies in Nottingham. Middle-class mothers breast-fed their babies more often than working-class mothers, and were no less inclined than the latter to 'demand feeding'. They checked the child's inclination to play with its genitals less often than working-class mothers, and less often smacked the child for 'naughtiness'.

But all this does not add up to a revolution in middle-class child-care methods to an unprecedented general permissiveness. Over many areas of behaviour, and in essence, middle-class child training remains ruthless. The Newsons found that in some respects middle-class mothers had high and inflexible expectations of their children: toilet training began earlier and was less casual; they were less inclined to soothe the baby to sleep ('There seems to be a strong middle-class feeling that babies should learn early to go to sleep at a "reasonable" hour without help and without making a fuss'); and while they are now much given to breast feeding, the dummy ('secondary oral gratification') finds little approval.

The working class seems to be less permissive principally in the sense that it is more inclined to resort to physical punishment. Middle-class discipline is more subtle, un-flinching and effective; working-class discipline is simply more desperate.

The most authoritative review of recent research in this field concluded that 'the most consistent finding . . . is the more frequent use of physical punishment by working-class parents. The middle class, in contrast, resort to reasoning, isolation, and . . . "love-oriented" discipline techniques.' 'Yet . . . it would be a mistake to conclude that the middle-class parent is exerting less pressure on his children.' 'Though more tolerant of expressed impulses and desires, the middle-class parent . . . has higher expectations for the child. The middle-class youngster is expected to take care of himself earlier, to accept responsibilities about the home, and—above all—to progress further at school.'[24]

The 'love-oriented' technique of discipline would be repugnant to many working-class parents; for in essence it is a tacit bargain between child and parents, love and affection given in return for good behaviour, withdrawn for misdeeds. Love is offered on strictly limited, contract terms. This appears from the cross-cultural surveys of anthropologists to be the most effective way of producing conscientious people prone to high guilt feelings and self-blame[25]—the very stuff of high academic promise.

Within the fringe of middle-class permissiveness exists a hard core of inflexible demand. Over many areas of be-haviour there is simply no question that things should be otherwise than parents decree or just quietly, tacitly assume. This applies not least to the age of school leaving and the type of school attended. When the author investigated the attitudes to education of parents in Leicester in 1960, working-class parents were inclined to say with regard to the choice of secondary school: 'Wherever he'll be happy.' Middle-class parents were quite clear on this issue, there was really no choice—the grammar school (or in some cases a public school) was the obvious place. 'Happiness' was an irrelevance.[26]

NEED-ACHIEVEMENT

The will to achieve—indeed the need to achieve—has its roots in family circumstances. Of particular importance are the child's relationships with its parents. If these are close, warm, and affectionate, he is likely to be handicapped for life.

Moralists in the past, Freudian psychologists today, and our own common sense, suggest that the young boy needs an adequate example and model in his father. The latter should be an effective human being with whom the boy can 'identify'. The evidence seems to be—in spite of Betty Spinley's *Deprived and the Privileged* and Madeline Kerr's *People of Ship Street*—that the moralists, Freudian psychologists, and common sense are wrong. The boy's long term interests are best served by an inadequate and feckless (if 'demanding') father.

Family relationships ('interaction patterns') have only quite recently been subjected to direct study and analysis for their bearing on children's development and achievement. There has long been a great deal of clinical evidence on family life, but this is of an indirect nature, drawn from patients' recollections of the often quite distant past. Of particular interest have been attempts to measure the strength of an individual's need for achievement (nAch) and to relate it to his family background. These attempts have not yet given a consistent and reliable picture and a great deal more work remains to be done. There is the further complication that high 'need-achievement' may not necessarily, for a wide variety of reasons, lead to actual achievement, at least in any specific field of endeavour.

Need-achievement has been measured by projective tests. Subjects write stories about pictures which are shown to them, and the stories are scored for their achievement imagery. The subjects, who have been aroused and put on their mettle by impressing on them the significance of the tests as indicators of their organizational abilities, will put their own hopes for success and fears of failure into their stories. But of course people hope for different kinds of success; and perhaps success for women is more typically in terms of getting on well with people, while for men it is getting on well in a career. Some individuals with high need-achievement scores may be indifferent to scholastic success, but hope for it in the sphere of athletics or the conquest of women. As one American investigator has pointed out: 'Motives have both force and direction. Present measures of need-achievement consider only the former while neglecting the latter.'[27] It is perhaps for this reason that general need-achievement scores have not been shown to relate very closely to success or failure at school.

Families of Jewish and Italian immigrants in America have been closely studied in an attempt to discover why children of the former tend to succeed at school and in their subsequent careers while children of the latter in general make poor progress.[28] It has been supposed that the subordination of the Italian child to the interests of the family might induce a sense of resignation and undermine the will to achieve. But Italian and Jewish fathers of similar occupational standing did not differ in the extent to which they expected children to be tied to their families. The investigators suggested—although the evidence is not really very firm—that very capable fathers produce a sense of helplessness in their sons, who feel they can never be masters of their own fate.

When family interaction processes were analysed, Italian fathers were found to give more support to their sons than Jewish fathers to theirs. The helpfulness of fathers seemed at best a mixed blessing: the fact that help is necessary tends to underline or suggest the son's incompetence. In line with this is the quite firm finding among American university students that people with high need-achievement scores perceive their parents as unfriendly and unhelpful. (Much may depend on the age of the person who is offered help. American high school pupils who are high in need-achievement do *not* see their parents as unhelpful.)[29]

The friendliness or unfriendliness of parents to their children of whatever age, their authoritarian or non-authoritarian attitudes, are perhaps an irrelevance. What matters is the independence they accord. The unhelpful parents, the non-authoritarian parent, the negligent parent, the ineffectual parent—all tend to be alike in this respect, that for no doubt quite different reasons they leave their children alone. But it is perhaps a help if, while leaving them alone, they also expect them in a general sense to do well.

Farmers in America make considerable demands on their children. Their expectations are detailed and specific; their control and guidance close. Perhaps for this reason farm families produce comparatively few successful children for non-farming careers. Farm boys have heavy demands made upon them for various kinds of achievement at a very early age; but the tasks are quite specific. In caring for livestock, milking and the like, they may have close guidance, help and instruction; but they have no freedom to explore, to shape their lives in their own way, to experiment with some degree of freedom in their growth towards independence.[30] Theirs is the opposite of the 'negative education' which Rousseau recommended before puberty. They need a good dose of neglect. As they then discovered for themselves a mastery of problematic situations, the confidence and will for achievement might be born.

To be left alone is perhaps one of the most urgent needs of children in a child- and home-centred society. (Studies of the careers of successful American scientists and scholars indicate that at some stage of their education their teachers have had enough sense to leave them alone. They have often suffered prolonged 'neglect', but in a general context of high expectation.) It is not only the kindly and tolerant parent who might, as a conscious decision, grant a child such freedom. 'The contrast should not be thought of too simply in terms of the autocratic–democratic dimensions, currently so popular in psychological literature.'[31] The important thing is that, for whatever reason, there is scope for 'the independent development of the individual'.

This may account for the high achievement, both scholastically and in professional careers, of men whose family relationships in youth were anything but warm and supportive. The men who have risen through education and their own efforts to the top of American business life perceive their early relationships with their fathers as at best detached, reserved, cool.[32] Fathers were often weak, inadequate and unreliable (although mothers were often strong and competent).

Perhaps such a childhood was a good preparation for the somewhat impersonal relationships of modern large-scale bureaucracy. The essential characteristic of these men in adult life was their independence. Similar rather detached and vague relationships with their parents seem to characterize the childhood of men who succeed in the physical sciences. Often in childhood they have had the experience of bereavement. Eminent social scientists have usually had a more stormy involvement with their parents, though scarcely more satisfactory from the point of view of psychology, humanity or common sense.[33] Neither humanity nor common sense seems to pay the highest dividends in the educational system and social order which we have devised.

A QUESTION OF CLASS

It is possible that our notion of the 'good home' needs to be redefined, or at least less naïvely defined. But there can be no doubt about the continuing influence of home background on educational and vocational advancement. In our contemporary democracy the influence of birth remains great and shows signs of increasing. Modern sociology and psychology are invoked to justify and promote enhanced parental power. Social science is used to support a position which social philosophy has discredited.

In less crude and direct ways than formerly, but no less effectively, parents have a powerful influence on the life-chances of their children. Their influence is particularly great in the intermediate ranges of ability, among border-line cases for selection and promotion. The outstandingly able will often make their own way whatever their family circumstances; and the outstandingly dull will have difficulty whatever backing they receive. But the great majority are neither outstandingly able nor dull; for them parents are often decisive.

The relationship between educational opportunity and attainment and 'social class' has been demonstrated often enough during the past decade. When middle-class children make use of the state system, they tend to get more grammar school places in proportion to their numbers than working-class children, to stay longer when they get to the grammar school, to be more involved in its extra-curricular activities, to have better examination results, to pass more often into the sixth form, and still more often to the university. Indeed, the further through the system we look, the more are children from white-collar and professional homes 'over-represented' in our grammar schools and institutions of higher learning.

There is no doubt that the children of skilled manual workers have benefited greatly from the 'scholarship system', particularly since 1944; but in the Ministry of Education's inquiry into early leaving in the nineteen-fifties they were somewhat under-represented in the grammar school intake at twelve, and more markedly under-represented in the sixth-form entry. (The children of skilled workers were 51 per cent of all children, 43·7 per cent of the grammar school entry at twelve, 37 per cent of the sixth-form entry. In contrast children of professional and managerial families were

15 per cent of all children, 25 per cent of the grammar school intake, 43·7 per cent of those entering the sixth form. Children of unskilled labourers were strikingly under-represented in the sixth form: they were only 1·5 per cent of the entry, but constituted 12 per cent of the age group.)

Although the general tendency is for children from the homes of manual labourers to deteriorate even when they enter the grammar schools, some do very well and exceed their initial promise. The Ministry's inquiry found that 12 per cent of these children who began in bottom streams had risen to top streams over five years. Although these children are, in general, a bad risk, it is a risk that must be taken: there is no way of telling which individuals will in fact do better than expected, and which will do worse.

The influence of family background operates today in more subtle ways than in the past—there is undoubtedly far less flagrant nepotism and patronage; but it is still very pervasive. The open competitive examination is the great social invention of the past century which has done most to eliminate it; and those who would abolish such examinations must face the certainty that the advantages of birth and family circumstances would be greatly enhanced.

With all its limitations and unfortunate side-effects, the open competitive examination for entrance into schools, universities and the public services is the main safeguard of the interests of people of humble origins, and our main guarantee of a measure of social justice. Only the lottery would remove altogether the advantages and disadvantages of birth. The open competitive examination remains the most effective instrument we have yet devised for the elimination of parents.

But they remain astonishingly potent. This is reflected in the high degree of self-recruitment still to be found in the major professions—and, indeed, in humbler employment, such as dockwork, where there may be special encouragement and opportunity for sons to follow in their fathers' footsteps. The sons of lawyers, doctors, parsons and teachers themselves become lawyers, doctors, parsons and teachers to a quite remarkable degree. In some professions this tendency to follow in father's footsteps has actually increased in a quite dramatic manner over the past century.

Only 6 per cent of Cambridge graduates who became teachers in the second half of the nineteenth century were the sons of teachers; in 1937–8, 14 per cent were teachers' sons. At both dates about a third of those who became doctors or parsons were the sons of doctors or parsons. Fifteen per cent of those entering law at the earlier date had lawyer fathers; in 1937–8, 26 per cent had lawyer fathers.[34] If we take a longer time span, over some two hundred years, the most remarkable change among Cambridge graduates is the extent to which the Church has become self-recruiting. In the eighteenth century the extent to which the sons of parsons became parsons barely exceeded what might happen by chance; by the nineteen-thirties they became parsons five times the chance expectation.[35]

Even in the academic world of twentieth-century Cambridge, where examinations and other objective tests of merit might be expected to have eliminated family influence, it is still a marked advantage in securing senior, or even junior, appointments to be a Macaulay, a Butler, a Trevelyan, a Huxley, or a member of the Wedgwood-Darwin connection, for example. The Provost of King's College, Cambridge, has analysed these intricate family alliances and has shown how once again, even at this level, the importance of having chosen the right father comes out at the borderline of ability (a very high borderline, of course, in this particular case).

> Clearly certain families produce a disproportionately large number of eminent men and women. But equally clearly the study shows that men of natural but not outstanding ability can reach the front ranks of science and scholarship and the foremost positions in the cultural hierarchy of the country if they have been bred to a tradition of intellectual achievement and have been taught to turn their environment to

account. Schools and universities can so train young men, but such a training has a far stronger command over the personality when it is transmitted through a family tradition. [36]

It is the task of schools in the second half of the twentieth century to achieve a similar command over the personalities entrusted to them even when the family has not done more than half their job for them.

VI

Satisfactions at Home, Club, Work and School

IN 1965 the author attempted to discover the personal needs which young people (between 14 and 20) in a northern industrial region expect their homes to meet, and the extent to which they think their needs are met. A complex of social institutions exists to meet the needs of young people: schools, youth clubs, and work make their contribution. The inquiry was designed to show the different kinds of demand made upon these different institutions, and the extent to which they provided satisfaction.

The relationship between the 'press' of institutions and personal needs has been systematically investigated in American colleges. Job-satisfaction in America has similarly been explored by comparing individual needs with the satisfaction provided by employment.[1] On a self-rating questionnaire the subject indicates the importance he attached to allegedly universal human needs such as 'Dominance', 'Recognition and Approbation', 'Dependence' and 'Independence'. He also indicates the levels of satisfaction in these various areas which he derives from his work. Need-strength can be compared with need-satisfaction.

The congruence or incongruence between personal needs and the practices and provisions of American colleges have been explored by Pace and Stern.[2] Again, the point of departure is supposedly universal human needs such as 'Achievement', 'Affiliation', 'Order', 'Sex' and 'Understanding'. The psychological needs of subjects are inferred from their responses on an 'Activities Index': they indicate their preferences 'among verbal descriptions of various

possible activities'. There are descriptions of orderly behaviour, dominant behaviour, deferential behaviour and so
on. On the College Characteristics Index subjects score true
or false corresponding descriptions of the college environment. Needs can then be compared with the perceived
satisfaction, pressures and demands of college life.

But needs are felt in relation to particular institutions. It
is true that an institution which manifestly aims to satisfy a
particular need may in fact satisfy others. But the boy who
goes to a youth club is unlikely to expect satisfaction of the
needs which are met through work, or to feel frustrated if
these latter needs are not met by the club. He may have a
great need for achievement which the club affords little
chance to satisfy; but he will not feel disgruntled, because
he never expected it to do so. The author decided to allow
spontaneous statements of need in relation to home, club,
school and work respectively. No prior assumptions about
needs were made: their nature would be determined only
after inspection of responses given in an open-ended
questionnaire. Satisfactions would be established from corresponding (spontaneous) statements about actual experience of the institutions in question.

Two-hundred-and-fifty members of 6 mixed youth clubs
in a northern conurbation completed usable questionnaires,
67 secondary school children who were not members of
youth clubs, and 50 young workers who were not club
members. The needs for which subjects sought satisfaction
at home were elicited by the following sentence openings:

> 'At home you *should* always have plenty of chance to . . .'
> 'First and foremost home *should* help you to . . .'
> 'At home you *should* always be able to feel that . . .'

The same three openings were applied to school, work and
club respectively. Corresponding cues were then provided
to elicit statements of actual satisfaction (or frustration):

> 'At home you always *have* plenty of chance to . . .'
> 'Above all else home *does* help you to . . .'
> 'At home you *do* feel that . . .'

Thus six statements were made by each subject about his home, his club, his school if he were still at school, or work if he were at work—a total of eighteen statements. Questionnaires were completed anonymously, but classificatory information was obtained and attached to each questionnaire: age, sex, type of education, age of leaving school or proposed age of leaving, examinations taken and passed, professional qualifications, type of employment (for those at work), and father's occupation.

There is an apparent danger that statements of needs are in reality statements of frustration; that the boy who writes, 'At home you should always have plenty of chance to express yourself,' says this precisely because he is given no such opportunity. The same difficulty arises in the 'need-press' analysis of Pace and Stern and the job-satisfaction inquiries of Schaffer. But the latter did not find a negative correlation between need-scores and satisfaction scores, and significant correlations have not been found between corresponding scores on the College Characteristics Index and the Activities Index.[3] In the inquiry reported here there was no significant tendency for statements of need to reappear in negative form in the second part of the questionnaire, as statements of dissatisfaction.

The type of projective test used in the present inquiry has the advantage that it does not present the subject with a perhaps arbitrary and possibly irrelevant list of 'needs' and 'satisfactions' which he is forced to reject or endorse. It has been fruitfully employed in America[4] and England;[5] and Symonds[6] found that a sentence-completion schedule not only supplemented personal data obtained in interviews, but was useful in correcting them. (Thus a report based on interview may describe a man as 'energetic'; responses on a projective test may show that a more accurate description would be 'nervous'.) It has the disadvantage that the need categories to which responses are assigned cannot be established in advance of the inquiry.

A coarse twofold classification of responses was made initially into 'expressive' and 'instrumental' categories. The distinction is taken from Talcott Parsons: 'Action may be oriented to the achievement of a goal which is an anticipated future state of affairs, the attainment of which is felt to promise gratification.' 'There is a corresponding type on the adjustive side which may be called *expressive* orientation. Here the primary orientation is not to a goal anticipated in the future, but the organization of a "flow" of gratifications (and of course the warding off of threatened deprivations).'[7] 'Problems of expressive interaction concern relationships with alters which ego engages in primarily for the immediate direct gratification they provide.'[8] By extension we refer not only to expressive and instrumental actions and functions, but to expressive and instrumental needs and satisfactions.

After scrutinizing all the responses six subdivisions which appeared logically distinct were made of the instrumental category, and seven of the expressive category. Two judges working independently were able to assign statements to these thirteen subgroups with virtually complete agreement. The instrumental category (I) was subdivided thus: (1) Intellectual skills, understanding and enlightenment; (2) Physical skills (including competence at games and sports); (3) Manual skills (including competence in domestic tasks); (4) Social skills (including poise and self-assurance in relationship with others); (5) Moral development (including references to 'forming a good character', 'becoming a good citizen', 'learning to be self-reliant and stand on your own feet'); (6) Personal advancement (including passing examinations, obtaining promotion, getting on in life).

The expressive category (E) was subdivided into: (1) Ease/emotional security (feeling at ease, wanted, loved, welcome); (2) Freedom/self-direction (including the freedom to express your views, have your say, 'be yourself'); (3) Friendship; (4) Sense of competence (including 'having a chance to prove yourself'); (5) Support from adults (including 'knowing that you can take your problems to parents/teachers/youth leaders'); (6) Sense of identity with the group ('feeling one of the crowd/a member of the family/ as if you belong'); (7) Sense of purposeful activity.

When the subjects who took part in the inquiry stated not what their institutions should, but did, provide, statements could be either positive or negative ('At home you always have a chance to relax', 'At home you always feel unwanted'). Statements referring to expressive satisfactions were divided into Expressive: Positive (E+) and Expressive: Negative (E—). The latter referred to (1) restrictions, constraints, humiliation, belittlement, rejection, and (2) boredom and demoralization.

The author first administered the questionnaire in six mixed youth clubs which were selected to represent different social areas within a large industrial conurbation. Two clubs were in well-to-do residential suburbs, two in working class districts, and two in socially mixed, transitional, areas. The clubs had a nominal membership of over 300. The clubs were given a week's notice of the author's visit. Club members co-operated well, and over 90 per cent of those present completed the questionnaire. Two-hundred-and-sixty-eight questionnaires were filled in; 18 were incomplete, illegible, or otherwise unusable; 250 were used in the analysis.

There were 135 males and 115 females. The age range was 14 to 20; 129 (51·6 per cent) were 16 years of age or over. One-hundred-and-sixty-three (65·2 per cent) came from the homes of professional and white-collar workers. Two hundred were still at school, 130 at grammar schools and 70 at modern schools. Sixty-seven of the grammar school pupils were in the sixth form. Twenty-four boys and 26 girls were at work. Twenty-nine of the workers had attended grammar schools and were all in non-manual, white-collar employment; 21 had attended secondary modern schools: the 8 boys were all in manual occupations, but 10 of the 13 girls were in routine non-manual employment, mainly as office workers.

For comparative purposes three classes of fourth-year pupils in three secondary schools in the areas served by the clubs were asked to complete the questionnaire. Sixty-seven of these boys and girls were not members of youth organizations. Fifty-seven (85·1 per cent) came from the homes of manual workers.

Fifty young workers between the ages of 16 and 20 were approached in recreational centres. They were not members of youth clubs or formal youth organizations. They were matched for age, sex and type of occupation with the 50 youth club members who were at work. Twenty-two of the 25 girls were in white-collar employment, 15 of the 25 boys. All 50 completed the questionnaire.

HOME

Both the expectations and satisfactions of home are predominantly 'expressive'. Two hundred-and-fifty club members made 750 statements about the needs which they expected home to satisfy, and 77·2 per cent of their statements referred to expressive satisfactions: being needed, feeling secure, having a chance to talk over personal problems with parents, and the like. Seven-hundred-and-fifty statements were made about the actual satisfactions of home: 72·3 per cent referred to expressive satisfactions.

In summary, the need-statements were: Expressive (E) 77·2 per cent, Instrumental (I) 22·8 per cent. The statements of satisfaction were: Expressive, positive (E+) 72·3 per cent, Expressive, negative (E−) 9·7 per cent, and Instrumental (I) 18·0 per cent.

Boys of all ages and girls over 16 place more stress on the instrumental functions of home than do younger girls. Twenty-nine point eight per cent of older girls' demands referred to instrumental needs, only 15·3 per cent of the younger girls' demands (CR 3·9, P < 0·001). The younger girls also find more dissatisfaction at home: 15·3 per cent of their statements refer to restrictions and other grievances, only 6·4 per cent of the older girls' statements (CR 8·3, P < 0·001).

Although there is a broad correspondence between needs and satisfactions, there are some major shifts within subcategories. While the greatest demand is for emotional security (approximately a third of all need-statements), this is closely followed by the demand for freedom and self-direction (approximately a quarter of all statements). The first demand is met in full, the second falls substantially short of satisfaction. Twenty-two point five per cent of the boys' demands and 23·9 per cent of the girls' referred to freedom and self-direction at home; only 13·3 per cent of the boys' stated satisfactions mentioned freedom and self-direction, and only 11·3 per cent of the girls' statements.

Nevertheless, home emerges on this sentence-completion schedule as a pre-eminently satisfying social institution for young people. This is in line with other inquiries into home life today. Inquiries among representative samples of English adolescents,[9] as well as comparative studies sponsored by Unesco,[10] indicate close bonds between young people and their parents and widespread appreciation of parents and reliance on them as guides and counsellors in times of trouble.

In the present inquiry tributes to parents were frequent at all social levels. Subjects often stated a desire to talk over problems with their parents, and as often stated that they were in fact able to do so. A 15-year-old daughter of a plumber wrote: 'At home you always feel you can tell your troubles to your parents and not be laughed at'; a 15-year-old son of a labourer: 'At home you always have a chance to tell someone your troubles'; a 16-year-old apprentice hairdresser, daughter of a textile buyer: 'At home you always have plenty of chance to talk sensibly to your parents'; a 17-year-old postman's daughter: 'At home you always feel that your opinions matter'; the 15-year-old son of a tailor: 'At home you always have plenty of chance to talk over matters with your parents'; the 15-year-old daughter of a fireman: 'At home you always have plenty of chance to air your views'.

Appreciation of home was expressed in more general, and often enthusiastic, terms. The 18-year-old daughter of a clerical worker wrote: 'At home you always feel confident that you are needed by someone'; the 16-year-old son of a shop manager: 'At home you always feel joyful'; the 14-year-old son of a bus driver: 'At home you always feel wanted and grateful to your mother'. Home offers relaxation, emotional security, and freedom to 'be yourself'. The 14-year-old daughter of a shopkeeper wrote: 'At home you always feel relaxed, unafraid, easygoing, and enjoying every minute of it'. (The same girl says of her grammar school: 'You always feel petrified of punishment and nervous of exams.') The 17-year-old son of a company director claimed that: 'At home you always feel happily unconscious of life'; the 16-year-old daughter of an engineer: 'Above all home helps you to have roots in a crazy world'. An 18-year-old typist, daughter of a civil servant, said that 'At home you always have plenty of chance to relax after work and you do not feel that you have to put on an act.'

At home you can be natural; individuality is recognized, a person is not an anonymous member of a larger social category. 'At home,' says the 14-year-old son of a manufacturer, 'you should be able to feel an individual in your own right.' Home should be, and is, a place where your opinions count. The 16-year-old son of a businessman was of the opinion that 'At home you should have plenty of chance to take part in things and have a say in things—like interior decoration (the colour of the wallpaper), to take one of many examples'. Such demands appear to be met. 'At home,' says the 17-year-old son of a salesman, 'you do feel that it really is a home, and not just a house you happen to live in.'

The instrumental purposes of home are overshadowed by the expressive; but more than 10 per cent of the expectations of home refer to moral training and character development, 'learning to stand on your own feet', 'becoming a responsible citizen', 'having a more sympathetic outlook toward others'. Table 1 shows the level of demand and satisfaction in this regard.

Social skills, manual skills and intellectual enlightenment are also sought at home, but to a smaller extent. About 3 per cent of the subjects looked for some form of intellectual understanding. 'Above all,' said a 17-year-old girl, 'home helps you to understand about adult things.' A 17-year-old boy thought that 'First and foremost home should help you to secure knowledge of things not taught at school, such as sex'. A general social competence is sometimes mentioned: 'Above all home helps you to manage your money and look after yourself' (18-year-old typist). 'Above all home helps you to learn how to live with people and how to be well

TABLE I

Statements about Moral Development
(Boys and Girls)

	Demand	Satisfaction
School (600)	9·8 %	6·0 %
Club (750)	4·0	4·4
Home (750)	12·1	7·8

NOTE: The figures in parentheses indicate the number of statements (or responses).

mannered' (18-year-old daughter of a clerical worker). The 14-year-old son of a bus driver claimed that: 'Above all home helps you to learn a lot about gardening.' For girls the instrumentality of home lies mainly in learning domestic skills: 'home helps you to learn about married life', and 'home helps you to learn how to run a home'.

Nine point seven per cent of statements about the actual experience of home expressed dissatisfaction or criticism (8·4 per cent of the boys' statements, 11·0 per cent of the girls'). Some references were made to being misunderstood (a 15-year-old girl, daughter of a Y.M.C.A. secretary, said: 'At home you feel that you're always in the wrong'; the 15-year-old son of a bingo hall manager said that at home 'you always feel that everyone is against you'). In the main grievances referred to restrictions and an overload of chores. 'At home you always feel that you must do a few jobs and bring home an unopened wage packet' said an 18-year-old laboratory assistant. An 18-year-old tripe dresser always has the urge, when at home, 'to be off all the time on my motorbike'. A 16-year-old trainee draughtsman 'always feels cooped up' at home; a 15-year-old engineer's daughter 'always feels in the way'; the 16-year-old daughter of a civil servant 'always feels helpless'. A 15-year-old girl, daughter of an insurance agent, always feels 'like an unpaid char'. Some—by no means entirely from working-class homes—complain of the lack of privacy at home. And the mass media are intrusive. Although some appreciate home as a place where television is constantly available (a 14-year-old boy appreciates the chance to 'loll around all the time with a cup of tea watching television'), others are like the 17-year-old son of a tailor who feels, at home, that he is 'televisionized, radioized, bookized, and newspaperized'.

Home is an enclosed world, isolated from wider social contacts, and largely accepted as such. The girls make some demand that they should be able to meet their friends at home (3·8 per cent of responses), but only 2·1 per cent mention home as a place where they do in fact meet their friends and non-family persons. Only 1 per cent of the boys mention home as a place where friends should or can be met. It is pre-eminently the club that is expected to meet the need for non-family contacts; and the need appears to be met in full.

THE YOUTH CLUB

Like home, the youth club is seen primarily in 'expressive' terms. It is not valued for any training it may provide in intellectual or even physical skills; in so far as it is instrumental, it is required to provide social training.

The needs which subjects hope the club would satisfy were: 82·9 per cent expressive, 17·1 per cent instrumental. The actual satisfactions were: E+ 78·3 per cent, E− 5·9 per cent, and I 15·8 per cent.

When the club was mentioned as a place to meet friends and be friendly with people, the statement was placed in the expressive category. ('Expressive action is not oriented to the attainment of a goal outside the immediate action situation and process itself in the same sense as is instrumental action' (Parsons, 1964).) When there was clearly a notion of learning to get on with people, developing one's social skills, the statement was placed in the instrumental class. In such statements the club was seen as a training situation, helping you to overcome shyness, gain social confidence and poise, learn how to mix and get on with people.

TABLE 2

Friendship and the Sense of Belonging
(Boys and Girls)

	Demand				Satisfaction			
	School (600)	Club (750)	Home (750)	Work (150)	School (600)	Club (750)	Home (750)	Work (150)
	%	%	%	%	%	%	%	%
Group solidarity	2·0	7·6	7·7	10·0	2·3	5·3	7·1	9·0
Ease and security	8·0	24·9	34·3	6·9	1·5	28·4	33·8	8·3
Friendship	4·7	23·8	2·3	8·6	4·5	21·7	1·6	9·3
TOTALS	14·7	56·3	44·3	25·5	8·3	55·4	42·5	26·3

NOTE: The figures in parentheses indicate the number of statements (or responses).

Above all club members demand from their clubs a sense of ease and emotional security. A quarter of their statements refer to feeling relaxed, at ease, wanted, welcome. A comparable number of statements refer to being friendly, meeting and making friends. Other statements refer specifically to a sense of group solidarity, feeling 'part of it', being 'one of the crowd'.

The demand for friendship often makes explicit mention of the opposite sex. Demands for specifically sexual contact or experience were rare, made by half a dozen boys. A 16-year-old grammar school boy thought that 'At the club you should have plenty of chance for sex'; another said that 'At the club you always feel sexy'; and a third 16-year-old boy said that 'At the club you always feel in a good and sexy mood'. Other-sex references were usually in less specifically sexual terms. A 14-year-old boy always feels happy at the club 'because of Valerie, Susan and Joan'. Sex antagonism as well as attraction was mentioned by three boys, thus: 'At the club you always feel opposed to the opposite sex' (a 16-year-old grammar school boy).

The club is expected to provide a place of refuge from the stress of life outside. Its main purpose is to offer compensation for the restrictions, anxieties and humiliations promoted by other institutions. It is an escape from the constraints of school and the surveillance of parents. 'At the club,' says the 14-year-old son of a solicitor, 'you should be able to feel relaxed and forget the terrible turmoil and distress of the world'. 'Above all the club helps you to get out of the school routine' (14-year-old grammar school girl).

Club membership legitimizes absence from home. 'Above all the club helps you to go out without my dad arguing' (14-year-old daughter of a lorry driver). It is an escape from parents: 'Above all the club helps you to do something constructive without criticism from parents: it is completely separate from parents' (17-year-old daughter of a senior civil servant). 'At the club you always feel that there is no-one there to snap at you' (14-year-old daughter of a lorry driver). 'At the club you should always be able to feel relaxed, without grown-ups nagging on to do this and not to do that' (15-year-old labourer's son). 'Above all the club helps you to get away from the washing up' (14-year-old architect's daughter).

At the club you should be able to express your views, have your say, put forward a point of view. Thirteen per cent of all demands were of this character; and 11 per cent of stated satisfactions were in those terms. Still greater demands of this nature are made of school and home, but satisfaction falls much further short of demand. (See Table 6.)

The club is expected to a greater extent than school or

home to provide training in social skills. 'First and foremost the club should help you not to be afraid of meeting people' (14-year-old modern school girl, daughter of a shopkeeper). 'The club should help you to talk to people more easily than you would otherwise' (15-year-old son of a chemist). 'First and foremost the club should help you to socialize' (17-year-old grammar school boy).

TABLE 3

Statements about Social Skills

	Demand	Satisfaction
School		
Boys (336)	2·9 %	1·8 %
Girls (264)	7·2	3·4
Club		
Boys (405)	8·1	5·2
Girls (345)	10·7	7·8
Home		
Boys (405)	2·7	1·0
Girls (345)	2·0	1·5

NOTE: The figures in parentheses indicate the number of statements (or responses).

Although the club is appreciated for the informal training in sociability which it affords, complaints are made of undue pressure from the leaders to 'mix in' and conform. The 16-year-old daughter of an engineer says that at the club she feels 'organized, frustrated, got-at, expected to conform, keep quiet, take part in ridiculous discussions, able to hike'. The 15-year-old daughter of a fishmonger feels that 'you're always expected to go along with everyone else'; the 15-year-old son of a bricklayer that 'you're always expected to do what the others are doing'.

Club leaders hope that the club will be far more instrumental than members want it to be. The questionnaire for members was modified for leaders. Twenty-seven leaders were asked to say what young people should have a chance to do at the club, in what ways the club should help them, and what, above all, they should feel when they were at the club. They were then asked what they thought, from their experience, young people did in fact look for in the club. They placed considerable stress on instrumental, mainly moral purposes; but when they considered reality, they recognized that 'expressive' purposes were predominant. (No club leader made an adverse comment on reasons for attending the club.)

TABLE 4

Function of the Youth Club
Statements by Leaders and Members

	Should		Is		
	E	I	E+	E—	I
Leaders (81)	53·1%	46·9%	74·0%	Nil	26·0%
Members (750)	82·9	17·1	78·3	5·9	15·8

NOTE: The figures in parentheses indicate the number of statements (or responses).

The 'instrumentality' that leaders hope for in the club is chiefly in the form of character training: teaching members to accept responsibility, to become useful citizens, to find a true sense of values, to achieve 'maturity'. They recognize that they come in the main to feel welcome, at ease, unconstrained and relaxed.

Of course some members valued the club in precisely the instrumental terms that leaders would approve. 'Above all,' said a 17-year-old grammar school boy, 'the club helps you to develop your administrative powers.' 'Above all the club helps you to learn self-discipline and human relations' (another 17-year-old grammar school boy). But the predominant demand was for current feelings rather than for future competence and personal development.

Statements expressing dissatisfaction with the club were few: 5·9 per cent of all statements made. Since the club is a voluntary association, this low proportion is not, perhaps, surprising. Dissatisfaction was almost wholly directed towards aimlessness and lack of clearly defined purpose: 'At the club you feel that you never do anything out of the ordinary and it is often boring.'

WORK

In the sentence-completion schedule completed by the 50 youth club members who were in full-time employment, work appeared to be generally satisfying, and in unexpected directions. The number of subjects in this group is, of course, small; and sub-groups (white-collar female workers, ex-grammar school boys, etc.) are too small to make reliable comparisons possible.

As one would expect, work was seen in instrumental terms to a far greater extent than home or club. But work was an instrument for other than crudely material ends: in fact, it is referred to largely as a learning situation (in a broad sense) by both manual and non-manual employees.

Forty-eight per cent of subjects' statements referred to expressive needs, 52 per cent to instrumental needs. Stated satisfactions were: E+ 45·3 per cent, E— 7·3 per cent, and I 47·4 per cent.

Boys and girls are alike in placing great stress on the educative value of work: understanding not only of techniques and processes, but of people and wider social problems should be promoted. Boys differ from girls in placing considerable stress on work as a means to 'getting on in life'. Girls look for friendship at work; but boys also place a high value on a sense of solidarity with the work group or organization.

'At work you always have plenty of chance to learn something new and to ask about things without being considered a nuisance,' says a 17-year-old trainee nurse. But it is not only trainees who appreciate work as education; indeed, for a 16-year-old apprentice electrician, work seems to mean, above all, a place 'where you are expected to put the kettle on at 9.55 sharp'.

It is the wider education in human affairs and understanding that receives most frequent mention: 'Above all work helps you to increase your knowledge of society' (16-year-old audit clerk); 'At work you always have plenty of chance to see how people react under the same conditions' (18-year-old male clerk); 'At work you always have plenty of chance to meet people and learn about different people' (15-year-old grocery assistant); 'Above all work helps you to be able to listen to older people's ideas and views' (18-year-old typist). And work promotes skill in human relationships: 'Above all work helps you to get on with other people' (18-year-old printing works operative).

Work is expected to develop 'character'. No less than 21 per cent of the demand is for moral training, in a broad sense. (On the other hand, only 11 per cent of subjects' statements about reality refer to satisfactions in this regard.) Work is expected to help you to become responsible, to learn to shoulder responsibility, to help you to 'grow up', to learn to 'stand on your own feet'. And in large measure it is seen as promoting a sense of responsibility, independence and self-reliance. Work 'helps you to prepare for responsibility later in life', says a 17-year-old office worker; 'above all work helps you to become a more mature person' (17-year-old fitter); 'Above all work helps you to rely on yourself' (17-year-old male shop assistant); 'Above all work helps you to have a life of your own, giving more independence than school did' (ex-grammar school clerical worker).

Fifteen per cent of the boys' statements demanded a sense of corporate membership at work; 11 per cent of their statements of satisfaction indicated that they achieved this sense of identification. (Only 5 per cent of the girls' demands and satisfactions referred to this sense of belonging to an organization or group.) 'At work you always feel part of the firm,' said a 19-year-old articled clerk; 'At work you always feel you are an essential part of the mechanism' (16-year-old bank clerk).

Seven point three per cent of the statements describing actual experience of work referred to frustrations and dissatisfactions. In no case was there any complaint about pay (except an oblique reference by a Post Office maintenance engineer: 'At work you always feel that it is a rich man's world').

A minority of statements referred to a sense of wasting time or being under undue pressure ('always feeling rushed off your feet'). A few statements referred to a sense of humiliation: 'At work you feel that some adults do not treat young people with any kind of respect' (18-year-old ex-grammar school girl employed as a clerk). 'At work you always feel you're being told what to do' (18-year-old operative in a printing works). But the broad picture which emerges is one of appreciation of work as an environment which fosters growth towards a self-confident and self-respecting maturity.

SCHOOL

Whereas home, youth clubs and work appeared substantially to meet the needs of young people in a northern conurbation, their schools did not. By far the highest proportion of negative statements were made on a sentence-completion schedule about school, particularly about the grammar school. Nineteen point five per cent of secondary modern school pupils' statements were negative; 32·8 per cent of grammar school pupils' statements were negative. (Pupils below the sixth form made 28·0 per cent negative statements, sixth formers 37·3 per cent.) By contrast, 9·7 per cent of the statements about home were negative, 5·9 per cent of statements about the club, and 7·3 per cent of statements about work.

In summary, the demands of modern school pupils were: Expressive (E) 57·1 per cent, Instrumental (I) 42·9 per cent. Their satisfactions were: Expressive, positive (E+): 32·4 per cent, Expressive, negative (E—): 19·5 per cent, and Instrumental (I): 48·1 per cent. The demands of grammar school pupils were: E 45·6 per cent, I 54·4 per cent. Their satisfactions were: E+ 23·6 per cent, E— 32·8 per cent, and I 43·6 per cent.

School is seen in an 'instrumental' light to a far greater extent than home or club. Grammar school pupils want it to be far more instrumental than modern school pupils: 54·4

TABLE 5

Statements about Intellectual and Physical Development
at School

	Demand	Satisfaction
All boys (336)		
Intellectual development	23·8 %	30·9 %
Physical development	4·2	4·0
All girls (264)		
Intellectual development	22·7	21·9
Physical development	0·4	1·5

NOTE: The figures in parentheses indicate the number of statements (or responses).

per cent of their demand is for instrumentality (chiefly in the sense of intellectual training, preparing for examinations, and helping one to get on in life) compared with 42·9 per cent of the modern school pupils' demand (CR 3·1, P < 0·01). But whereas grammar school pupils mention instrumental satisfactions less frequently than they mention instrumental expectations (43·6 per cent compared with 54·4 per cent), modern school pupils mention them more often (48·1 per cent compared with 42·9 per cent). Grammar school pupils appear to get less instrumentality than they desire, modern school pupils appear to get a surfeit.

Intellectual training and preparation for a career over-shadow all other instrumental demands and satisfactions. It is not only the grammar school pupils who want to learn.

Thus a 15-year-old modern school girl, daughter of a warehouseman, says: 'At school you always have plenty of chance to have things explained which you don't understand.' More commonly they make general statements to the effect that at school you have plenty of chance to learn and 'get a good education'. The opportunity to develop physical skills is mentioned much less frequently by both grammar school and modern school pupils.

TABLE 6

Statements about Freedom and Self-direction
(Boys and Girls)

	Demand	Satisfaction	d
School			
Boys (336)	22·0%	3·6%	−18·4%
Girls (264)	22·3	8·3	−14·0
Club			
Boys (405)	13·5	10·4	− 3·1
Girls (345)	13·3	11·0	− 2·3
Home			
Boys (405)	22·5	13·3	− 9·2
Girls (345)	23·9	11·3	−12·6

NOTE: The figures in parentheses indicate the number of statements (or responses).

It is in its expressive rather than its instrumental role that school falls far short of demand. The major expressive demand is for freedom and self-direction: freedom to put your own point of view, to be treated as an individual. This is also a major demand of club and home; but these institutions appear to come nearer than the school to satisfying the demand.

Both modern school and grammar school pupils express their appreciation of school as a social institution. 'At school you always feel needed and part of the school,' says a 14-year-old grammar school boy. 'At school you always have a chance to talk to the staff relatively freely,' says a 16-year-old grammar school girl. A 15-year-old modern school girl says that 'Above all school helps you to feel adult'; the 14-year-old son of a truck driver says that 'At school you always feel that you are some one, even if you aren't'. Another modern school boy expresses a similar sentiment: 'At school,' he says, 'you always feel that you are somebody.' 'At school,' says a 15-year-old modern school girl, 'you always feel that the teachers are interested in you.'

Like grammar school pupils, modern school pupils also make negative statements, chiefly about restrictions and personal humiliations. 'At school,' says the 15-year-old daughter of a boiler-man, 'you always feel that you cannot do what you want and that teachers are against you.' (At home the same girl finds the freedom she wants: 'You always have plenty of chance to do what you like. You're not told to stop talking, like at school.')

Another 15-year-old girl says that at school 'you always feel boxed in, regimented, treated like the second form, and angry at the lack of trust'. The 15-year-old daughter of a clerk says of her modern school that 'you always feel that you're still a child. They should encourage you to grow up.' (She, too, finds freedom at home, where 'you always feel loved and highly thought of'.) Modern school boys are more likely than grammar school boys to refer to physical humiliations: 'At school you always feel that teachers can pull your hair and slap you at the back of the neck.'

But grammar school pupils differ significantly from modern school pupils in the frequency of their unfavourable comments about school. It is difficult to explain this simply as a function of higher intelligence and critical powers: grammar school pupils do not exercise their superior intelligence in this way when they make comments on their home, club, and work. There is no tendency for working-class pupils in grammar schools to make more negative statements than pupils from middle-class homes.

There was a tendency for sixth formers to be more negative than pupils below the sixth form, but the difference falls short of significance at the 5 per cent level. The sixth formers who took part in this inquiry were not borderline academics. The boys had obtained an average of 6 O-level G.C.E. passes, the girls 7. Some had already distinguished themselves in A-level examinations and were staying on for a third year in the sixth.

TABLE 7

Statements of Satisfaction and Dissatisfaction with School
(Boys and Girls)

	'School is'		
	E+	E—	I
Modern school (210)	32·4%	19·5%	48·1%
Grammar school (390)	23·6	32·8	43·6

Chi square 10·18   d.f.2   P < 0·01

NOTE: The figures in parentheses indicate the number of statements (or responses).

The great demand is for self-expression and self-direction: 'At school you should have plenty of chance to express your views'; 'At school you should always be able to feel that masters are not simply disciplinarians'. And one should be recognized and treated as an individual: 'At school you should be able to feel that you are a human being and not just a "B" pupil' (14-year-old barrister's daughter).

To a large extent the nine grammar schools contributing to the research population appeared to be failing to meet this demand. 'At school you always feel like a little boy' (15-year-old son of a clothing manufacturer); 'At school you always feel disgusted with life' (15-year-old son of a school-master); 'At school you always feel looked down on by masters' (18-year-old son of an advertising agent). The dissatisfaction does not arise from expectations of an easy time which is denied them: a 17-year-old tailor's son says that at school you should feel expected 'to work hard and diligently'; but he feels 'neglected, sick, tired, bored, disgusted and generally miserable'.

The 18-year-old son of a branch manager of an insurance company 'always feels downgraded' at school; the 14-year-old son of a manufacturer's agent 'always feels a prisoner'. The 15-year-old son of a pharmacist finds that at school 'you always have a chance to be just one of a conformist rabble: at school you always feel unimportant and hounded'. (At home, by contrast, he says he has 'plenty of chance to be an individual'.) The 15-year-old son of a furniture manu-

TABLE 8

Dissatisfactions of Sixth Formers

	E+	E−	I
Sixth formers (201)	24·4%	37·3%	38·3%
Pupils below the Sixth (189)	22·8	28·0	49·2

Chi square 5·35   P < 0·10

NOTE: The figures in parentheses indicate the number of statements (or responses).

facturer says that 'at school you always feel like a chicken which is being stuffed'. (He also finds happier circumstances at home, where 'you always have plenty of chance to talk over your difficulties with your parents'.)

The sense of losing one's individuality in an anonymous organization is felt at all levels of seniority. An 18-year-old boy says that at school 'you always feel restricted and socially unstable, obliged to follow all lines of authority with no expression of radical thought'. The 18-year-old son of a joiner feels that 'you have to try hard to preserve your individuality'; the 17-year-old daughter of a tailor feels 'disgusted that teachers do not take enough interest in the individual'; the 16-year-old son of an insurance agent always feels 'boxed, and one of a crowd'; the 15-year-old son of a civil servant feels 'part of a huge system'.

The pressure of work and the aloofness and authoritarian

attitudes of staff are mentioned as well as the impersonality of the organization. 'At school you always feel victimized,' says a 17-year-old sixth former, son of a manufacturer's agent. It is perhaps more understandable that at 13 the daughter of an accountant should 'always feel under their thumb'.

A 15-year-old girl says she always feels as if she's in prison, 'expected to obey the rules without questioning'. The 16-year-old daughter of a principal viola player finds that 'at school you always have plenty of chance to listen to your teacher's opinions' and 'you always feel bored'. (By contrast, at home 'you always have plenty of chance to discuss things with your family', and 'home helps you to develop your own interests'.) At school, says the 15-year-old daughter of a wool-sorter, 'you always feel that you are inferior to teachers—that is what they would like you to think'. And at school you are expected to 'work, work, work'.

The 16-year-old son of a university lecturer echoes this sentiment: 'At school you always have plenty of chance to slog, slog, slog, and to be treated like a kid who must not ask awkward questions.' In his case home brings no relief: 'at home you always feel ignored'. The club appears to be his only salvation: 'at the club you always feel that you're enjoying yourself.'

It may be the pressure and restrictions of the grammar school that account for the over-representation of grammar school pupils in youth clubs. This, of course, is only speculation; but when we look at the pattern of expectation and satisfaction around home, school, club and work, it is possible to see how deprivations in one institution appear to find alleviation in another. Where school fails to satisfy, home or club may satisfy abundantly.

Tables 9 and 10 present in summary form the frequency of statements in the 13 major need categories. Dominant needs or satisfactions, which are indicated by heavy type, are those categories which contain more than one-thirteenth of all statements.

TABLE 9

Boys' Statements of Need and Satisfaction
(Percentages)

	Demand				Satisfaction			
	School (405)	Club (336)	Home (405)	Work (72)	School (405)	Club (336)	Home (405)	Work (72)
	%	%	%	%	%	%	%	%
Intellectual	**23·8**	0·2	2·9	**13·9**	**30·9**	0·5	3·4	**13·9**
Physical	4·2	2·4	Nil	1·4	4·0	4·2	0·5	1·4
Manual	Nil	Nil	0·7	1·4	Nil	0·5	0·7	2·8
Social	2·9	**8·1**	2·7	Nil	1·8	5·2	1·0	1·4
Moral	9·8	4·7	**12·8**	**19·4**	5·0	5·4	9·1	**13·9**
Advance-ment	**10·1**	0·6	5·2	**16·6**	9·5	0·3	3·9	**11·1**
Emotional security	8·0	24·9	34·3	6·9	*1·5*	28·4	33·8	8·3
Freedom	22·0	**13·5**	22·5	5·6	*3·6*	10·4	**13·3**	*2·8*
Friendship	3·9	**22·7**	1·0	7·0	2·6	21·5	1·2	**9·7**
Sense of compet-ence	2·9	1·5	1·2	0·7	1·5	1·2	2·4	**8·3**
Support from adults	2·6	Nil	5·9	2·8	1·8	0·5	5·2	Nil
Identity with group	2·1	**8·9**	7·4	**15·3**	2·9	*3·7*	5·2	**11·1**
Sense of purpose	4·5	**10·3**	1·0	4·2	3·0	**10·1**	1·7	**5·5**
Negative state-ments					20·2	5·2	8·4	5·5

NOTE: Heavy type indicates major demand or satisfaction. Italics indicate half or less of the demand. Figures in parentheses indicate the number of statements (or responses).

TABLE 10

Girls' Statements of Need and Satisfaction
(Percentages)

	Demand				Satisfaction			
	School (264)	Club (345)	Home (345)	Work (78)	School (264)	Club (345)	Home (345)	Work (78)
	%	%	%	%	%	%	%	%
Intellectual	22·7	0·6	2·9	14·2	21·9	1·7	3·7	15·4
Physical	0·4	0·3	Nil	Nil	1·5	2·3	Nil	2·6
Manual	Nil	0·3	3·2	2·6	Nil	Nil	1·7	5·1
Social	7·2	10·7	2·0	3·6	*3·4*	7·8	1·5	*1·3*
Moral	9·2	2·1	11·3	23·1	7·2	2·1	6·4	*8·9*
Advancement	8·7	0·6	3·7	9·0	*2·3*	0·3	*2·3*	14·1
Emotional security	8·0	21·4	31·0	9·0	5·3	20·6	33·3	9·0
Freedom	22·3	13·3	23·9	7·7	*8·3*	11·0	*11·3*	6·4
Friendship	5·7	28·1	3·8	10·3	6·8	22·0	2·1	9·0
Sense of competence	4·5	1·7	2·0	5·1	4·2	1·1	1·1	6·4
Support from adults	2·3	0·6	4·6	7·7	1·5	0·3	5·8	Nil
Identity with group	1·9	6·1	8·1	5·1	1·5	7·2	9·3	6·4
Sense of purpose	2·6	11·0	0·3	9·0	3·0	11·9	1·1	5·1
Negative statements					29·5	5·5	7·7	10·3

NOTE: Heavy type indicates major demand or satisfaction. Italics indicate half or less of the demand. Figures in parentheses indicate the numbers of statements (or responses).

CLUB MEMBERS AND NON-MEMBERS

Youth club members are probably unrepresentative in various ways of the general population of young people between 14 and 20 years of age. Young people who are attending or have attended grammar schools appear to be members more often, in proportion to their numbers, than modern school pupils. From the evidence collected for the Crowther Report (1960),[17] 'It seems evident that, in respect

TABLE 11

Statements by Club Members and Non-members about School
(Percentages)

	Demand		Satisfaction		
	E	I	E+	E−	I
Non-members (201)	44·7	55·2	39·8	8·0	52·2
Club members attending modern schools (210)	57·1	42·9	32·4	19·5	48·1

Chi square 12·0   d.f.2   P < 0·01

NOTE: The figures in parentheses indicate the number of statements (or responses).

of length of active membership, the boys from selective schools made an appreciably better showing throughout every type of youth organization than did others.' It seems possible, on the face of it, that clubs attract the 'clubbable', the more socially responsible and amenable of the teenage population.

In order to provide a rough check on the possible divergence of attitudes between the club members in this survey and other young people of similar age, schooling and occupation, a group of last-year secondary school pupils, and a group of young people at work, none of whom were club members, were invited to complete the appropriate sections of the questionnaire. The young workers were approached at recreational centres which were not youth organizations in any formal sense.

A last-year class in each of three mixed secondary schools in the areas served by the clubs completed the questionnaire. Sixty-seven pupils (33 girls and 34 boys) were not members of clubs. Their average age was 15 years. Eighty-five per cent came from the homes of manual workers, 15 per cent from white-collar homes.

TABLE 12

Statements by Club Members and Non-members about Home
(Percentages)

	Demand		Satisfaction		
	E	I	E+	E—	I
Non-members (201)	76·1	23·9	80·6	1·5	17·9
All club members (750)	77·2	22·8	72·3	9·7	18·0

Chi square 46·0   d.f.2 P < 0·001

NOTE: The figures in parentheses indicate the number of statements (or responses).

These 67 non-members were less negative in their attitude to school than club members of the same age who were attending the same type of school. Their demands of school were substantially the same, but their satisfaction with school was significantly different.

There was a similar difference in attitude to home. Non-members had the same expectations as members, but they made a significantly lower proportion of negative and critical statements.

Fifty young workers (25 men and 25 women) between the ages of 16 and 20, who were not members of clubs, completed the questionnaire. Fifteen men were white-collar workers, 10 were manual workers; 22 women were in white-collar employment, 3 in manual. In their attitude to work they did not differ from the club members who were in full-time employment: 8·0 per cent of their statements about work were negative, 7·3 per cent of club-members' statements.

But they were far less negative in their attitudes to home. Only 2 per cent of their statements were negative, compared with 8·2 per cent of statements made by club members of their age.

These results suggest that the youth club, far from attracting the less recalcitrant young people of the area, provides a refuge for those who feel more resentment towards their homes than other young people. This should not be interpreted as indicating that the homes of club members are generally 'unsatisfactory' and severely deprived. Club members in general are highly appreciative of their homes, but to a rather less marked extent than the non-members who completed the questionnaire.

SELF-CONCEPTS IN A GRAMMAR SCHOOL

The negative attitudes of grammar school pupils in general, and of senior pupils in particular, towards their schools, seemed to call for further investigation and, if possible, verification. If frustration of 'expressive' needs is as widespread and severe as the survey seemed to indicate, it would be reasonable to expect that grammar school pupils, particularly in the upper school, would be characterized by generally negative self-concepts. The self-concepts of first formers and sixth formers were accordingly investigated in an apparently 'typical' grammar school.

The school had not contributed any subjects to the original research population. It is a three-form entry mixed grammar school, recruiting pupils on the basis of selection tests at the age of eleven. It is a well established school with a good academic record.

Charles Cooley[11] and G. H. Mead[12] argued that a person's self-conception is derived from the way others define him and from the various positions he occupies in society. Mead stressed the importance of the 'generalized other', the individual's conception of the organized social process of which he is part. If senior grammar school pupils in fact feel 'downgraded', 'unimportant and hounded', as some had alleged, we should expect this experience to be reflected in their self-conception.

Sarbin[13] defined the self-concept as the sum of a person's self-perceptions, and argued that it could be discovered by asking subjects to indicate their qualities and characteristics on an adjective check-list. More recent work on the self-concept has included the subject's perceptions not only of himself but of others, 'A person's psychological field, his formulation of the world.'[14] The W–A–Y test developed by Bugental and Zelen[15] explores the self-concept in this wider sense.

TABLE 13

Boys' Self-concepts:
Statements by First and Sixth Formers

	Negative	Positive	Neutral
First form (840)	11·9%	28·2%	59·9%
Sixth form (620)	30·2	28·0	41·8

Chi square 82·3   d.f.2 P < 0·001

NOTE: The figures in parentheses indicate the number of statements (or responses).

Bugental and Zelen asked subjects to provide three answers to the question, 'Who are you?' They established 17 response categories into which answers could be placed. Kuhn and McPortland[16] used the same procedure but required 20 answers to their question. The author used the Kuhn and McPortland test with his grammar school subjects and classified the responses according to a slightly modified version of the response categories which have been used by other investigators. Subjects completed the test anonymously (although a small proportion nevertheless gave their names in answering the question).

The test was administered to 141 subjects, 90 in the first form (42 boys and 48 girls) and 51 (31 boys and 20 girls) in the upper sixth. Seventy subjects came from the homes of manual workers, 71 from white-collar homes.

The 17 response categories fall into a broad threefold classification: (1) neutral statements, (2) affectively toned negative statements, and (3) affectively toned positive statements. Affectively toned statements may refer to self or to other people and external situations.

The self-concepts of sixth formers were far more negative than the self-concepts of first formers. The discrepancy was greater in the case of boys than of girls.

TABLE 14

Girls' Self-concepts:
Statements by First and Sixth Formers

	Negative	Positive	Neutral
First form (960)	14·3 %	30·7 %	55·0 %
Sixth form (400)	26·7	35·3	38·0

Chi square 42·6 d.f.2 P < 0·001

NOTE: The figures in parentheses indicate the number of statements (or responses).

Sixth form boys made more affectively toned, and fewer neutral, statements than first formers; the shift from neutral statements was entirely in the direction of negative comment. The same trend was apparent among the girls. There were no social class differences in the proportions of negative statements.

Sixth form girls were not less negative than sixth form boys: their 26·7 per cent negative statements are not significantly different from the 30·2 per cent of the boys (CR 1·32, NS).

The first formers (they had spent two terms in the school) defined themselves in terms of their likes and enthusiasms, their membership of social groups and organizations. The sixth formers' self-concept was characterized by hatred of self and of others; by non-reference to membership groups. First formers tended to define themselves in terms of a geographical location, sixth-formers did not. First formers saw themselves in physical terms; sixth formers (and girls even less than boys) seldom referred to their appearance. First formers referred to their family relationships more often than sixth formers; first form boys mentioned their age more often than sixth form boys. Sixth formers defined themselves in terms of socio-political affiliations (political parties, C.N.D. and the like) more often than first formers. There was no difference in the proportions of religious and metaphysical self-descriptions.

A half of the sixth form boys said they were drinkers and/or smokers; a third referred to their lack of money. A half of the sixth form boys referred to sex or members of the opposite sex: 'I am sexually frustrated'; 'I am in love'; 'I like short dark girls'; 'I have had sex'. Only two of the 20 sixth form girls made any reference whatsoever to the opposite sex (but a quarter of the girls said they were fond of children). One of the girls made three references to sex: 'I am in love/I am in a personal dilemma concerning sex: is it always wrong before marriage? and is 18 too young to become engaged?/I am conscious of the fact that sometimes I do not love my boy friend, and more often he does not love me.' A third of the boys at all ages and a sixth of the girls describe themselves as intelligent or highly intelligent. Tables 15 and 16 show the proportion of statements in the various response categories and the significance of the difference between first and sixth formers.

First form pupils made far more (neutral) statements which were impossible to classify in the established categories (see 'undesignated: neutral' responses). The self percepts of sixth formers were far more homogeneous than the self percepts of first formers. The latter tended more often to describe themselves in unclassified ways, such as 'I am a Leo subject', 'I am a vegetarian', 'I am a person without an appendix'. (Medical histories figured in their self-conceptions, almost never in sixth formers': 'I am a dentist hater',

'I am always having colds', 'I am a doctor hater', 'I am on a hospital waiting list'.)

Religion was not prominent at any age with either sex;

TABLE 15

Statements Made in the W–A–Y Test by Grammar School Boys

Statement categories	First form (840)	Sixth form (620)	Difference	
			C.R.	P
A. NEUTRAL	%	%		
Name	2·5	0·3		
Pronoun	0·7	0·3		NS
Social–scientific	1·5	0·3	2·3	0·05
Metaphysical	0·1	0·3		NS
Sex	4·5	3·5		NS
Age	3·6	1·7	2·1	0·05
Occupation (future)	1·5	3·7	2·6	0·01
Family relationship	5·0	1·2	4·0	0·001
Group status/membership	10·1	4·3	4·1	0·001
Geographical-spatial	4·9	1·0	4·1	0·001
Socio-political	0·1	5·5	6·5	0·001
Nationality	1·5	2·5		NS
Religion	1·5	2·7		NS
Appearance	7·2	3·5	3·0	0·01
Neutral: undesignated	15·0	11·0	2·1	0·05
B. AFFECTIVELY TONED				
Negative	11·4	30·2	8·5	0·001
Negative-self	7·2	22·1		
Negative-nonself	4·2	8·1		
Positive	28·2	28·0		NS
Positive-self	11·4	17·4		
Positive-nonself	16·8	10·6		

NOTE: The figures in parentheses indicate the number of statements (or responses).

but in one or two cases it dominated the self-image. A 12-year-old girl described herself as 'one of God's children/a sinner in God's name/a chosen person of God/a member of the congregation of the Central Methodist Church/a member of the Sunday school'. (She is also a Girl Guide and hopes to go to a university to study sociology.)

TABLE 16

Statements Made in the W–A–Y Test by Grammar School Girls

Statement categories	First form (960)	Sixth form (400)	Difference C.R.	P
A. NEUTRAL	%	%		
Name	3·5	Nil		
Pronoun	0·5	0·8		NS
Social–scientific	1·5	2·6		NS
Metaphysical	0·2	0·8		NS
Sex	3·4	3·5		NS
Age	3·2	2·0		NS
Occupation (future)	2·2	4·0		NS
Family relationship	5·4	2·3	1·96	0·05
Group status/membership	9·7	6·3		NS
Geographical–spatial	3·0	0·8	2·3	0·05
Socio-political	0·2	3·4	6·5	0·001
Nationality	1·1	0·3		NS
Religion	2·0	2·3		NS
Appearance	5·1	1·5	3·0	0·01
Neutral: undesignated	14·0	7·4	6·3	0·001
B. AFFECTIVELY TONED				
Negative	14·3	26·7	5·2	0·001
Negative-self	8·0	24·0		
Negative-nonself	6·3	2·7		
Positive	30·7	35·3	2·4	0·05
Positive-self	7·3	15·5		
Positive-nonself	23·4	19·8		

NOTE: The figures in parentheses indicate the number of statements (or responses).

Negative self-references in the first form refer more often than in the upper sixth to personal appearance and performance in school subjects and other school activities. 'I am lumpy/I am plain'; 'I am not a very good swimmer/not a very brave person/frightened of the dentist/not very good at making friends quickly/not very good at making conversation'. Social uncertainty is apparent here, but is still more prominent six years later. A first form boy sees himself as 'a show-off/weak willed/always in trouble/rotten at French/hopeless at cross-country running/a lazy person really/dim compared with my friend/untidy/fed up with my sister'. But much more commonly at this age the self-conception is predominantly positive: 'I am very lucky to have such a good home/I am much indebted to my grandparents for what they have done for me/I am very fond of the countryside/I am a lover of cats/I am a lover of snow, ice and camping out'.

There is little joy in the upper sixth. Only one predominantly positive self-image emerged, with positive statements outnumbering negative. This was a girl who saw herself as 'a highly intelligent person/interesting/a poet/unique/in love with life/glad I am myself/self-confident/a person who usually succeeds'. But even she concedes: 'I am often rather snobbish/I am inclined to attempt too much at once'.

The following excerpts illustrate the negative content of 10 sixth form boys' self-conceptions:

1. 'I am unsure of my abilities/afraid of failure/a person who needs many friends/concerned about my A-levels/worried about my girl/selfish'. On the other hand he thinks he is 'lucky/tall, and stronger than most/fond of drink and women'.

2. 'I am greedy/self-centred/weak willed/vain/unable to accept the world/shoddy in appearance/full of self pity/ashamed of myself'. But he also sees himself as 'intelligent/kind/generous/in love'.

3. 'I am against old people, coloured people, Jews/I find most adults annoying/I hate my father/I do not think young people owe their parents anything/I hope never to live to be an old man/I hate zoos and circuses'. But he 'drinks, and smokes 90 cigarettes a week' and 'has had sex'.

4. 'I am dissatisfied with my present social status/worried

about my future/disliked by a large portion of the lower school/feel lonely at school/am not skilled at anything/not a member of a club of any sort/not attractive in appearance/looking forward to leaving school'. He is a Conservative in politics and has 'several high but improbable ambitions'.

5. 'I am against coloured immigrants/I am anti-Yank/an agnostic'. (But he, too, is a drinker and a smoker and attracted by women.)

6. 'I am a coward/lazy/quick tempered/a hater of cats'.

7. 'I am afraid of being physically crippled' (but he is 'fond of short dark girls').

8. 'I am frightened by loneliness/I am even more frightened by large social gatherings/I am disgusted with other people's self-confidence/pessimistic by nature/tempted and lack will power/a bad loser/in many ways a hypocrite/undecided concerning hanging and euthanasia/a church member who feels wholly inadequate'.

9. 'I am in favour of the colour bar/a person who would not stand out in a crowd/rather lazy/a person who looks down on Communists'.

10. 'I am a segregationist/I am disappointed with many aspects of my life'. But he's a drinker and a smoker and (perhaps for this reason) 'a person not in the best of health'.

The girls were similar in their self-appraisal. The following is illustrative material:

1. 'I am easily depressed/in a rut/afraid of death/mixed up as regards my religious beliefs/unable to relax/dissatisfied with my present station in life'. On the other hand, she says she is intelligent and hopes to go to college.

2. 'I am sometimes afraid/uncertain about the future/happiest when I forget about my present life/able to forget by singing or playing a musical instrument/shy till I get to know people/hoping to pass my exams, but don't think I will/afraid of lots of things, like the dark/happy to sit in front of a roaring fire rather than go out.'

3. 'I am anxious over exams/not glamorous/not very kind to human beings, but kind to animals'.

4. 'I am hopeless at making decisions/not very good at ordering people about, because they take no notice of me/I am dithery'. (But she likes peanuts, liquorice, and the sea.)

5. 'I am often very depressed/conscious of a desire to be popular/hoping to go to the university, but scared at the prospect'.

6. 'I am uncertain about the future/afraid of death/extremely lazy/extremely plain'. (But she is 'a good cook' and 'very partial to Vodka'.)

7. 'I am a pessimist/an introvert, unfortunately/a basically shy person/a highly strung person/a very moody person'. She intends to be a teacher.

8. 'I am selfish/a snob/too fond of the limelight/lazy/inconsistent'. She intends to be a teacher, too.

This inquiry suggests that home and work may be meeting the needs and expectations of young people to a greater extent than is often supposed; and that the grammar school, particularly in its higher reaches, may often be failing to promote the self-confident and assured maturity which is often supposed to develop from sixth form experience. There were no indications in this inquiry that there is, in general, a great gulf between teenage children and their parents; that they are unable to communicate; that children throughout their teens do not place high value on their parents' support and approval. All the evidence is to the contrary. Between 14 and 20, the young people attending six northern youth clubs—and other groups who were not members of clubs—in general appeared to appreciate their homes and to find in them ease, relaxation and reassurance.

Youth clubs do not appear to be the arenas of strenuous self-improvement which youth leaders would like them to be; but they offer a sense of release and relaxation which other institutions provide less abundantly. They are also valued for the opportunity they afford for developing social skills and extending one's social horizons.

Any interpretation of grammar-school pupils' negative attitudes to school can only be speculative. The grammar school measures up to the considerable demands for intellectual development and personal advancement. But it is seen as a largely restrictive institution, and many pupils appear to find staff–student relationships remote and chilling even in the sixth form.

The negative self-concepts of sixth formers are in line with this picture. The developed critical powers of senior pupils might be held to account for their comparatively unfavourable view of themselves and their schools. But they do not view their homes and clubs less favourably than younger or less intelligent people. And the hostile comments which appeared in the W–A–Y test were often more suggestive of blinkered, stereotyped thinking (for example with regard to coloured immigrants and other social problems) than of an enlightened, radical and informed reappraisal of life and society.

The sixth form probably tends to select negative and introverted personalities. Their negative and introverted characteristics are perhaps reinforced by their experiences. Negative self-concepts may be a necessary price of high academic attainment under highly competitive conditions. And it may be the case that some discrepancy between expressive needs and expressive satisfactions constitutes a creative tension. But there is probably a point beyond which this tension ceases to be creative and becomes demoralizing.

No attempt was made in this inquiry to relate expressive need-frustrations to academic performance. There was no indication in these data that those who were most critical of school came from the 'poorer' schools, with generally lower attainment; there were, indeed, some signs that the reverse was true. Numbers were not large enough to make inter-schools comparisons possible; but there appeared to be a tendency for pupils from large grammar schools of high academic distinction, recruiting their pupils in the main from higher professional families (there were four such schools contributing subjects) to be particularly negative in their attitudes. The inquiry did not begin as a research into the personal consequences of an advanced academic education. But the material which emerged suggests that grammar schools which differ in their size, social composition and academic distinction might be usefully compared for the attitudes and self-conceptions which they induce in their pupils.

On the wider issue of family influence on young people, with which this book is centrally concerned, the inquiry reported above must be seen alongside the growing body of work which casts serious doubts on the widespread 'rejection' of parental values and guidance by adolescents. This work comes from all parts of the advanced Western world, from North America as well as from more apparently conservative and traditional countries. Thus recent research in suburban Montreal led to the inescapable conclusion that:

> the adolescents, by the age of 14 and 15, have already internalized the ideals and values of the surrounding adult society. The adolescent appreciates the keen interest of the parents in their activities and feel that their parents are working on their behalf; they are in close agreement with their parents on general career and marriage goals and the manner in which these goals are to be achieved . . . they do not reject adult values or participate in an anti-adult "youth culture". . . .'[18]

Those who are concerned with the maintenance of traditional values may find some reassurance in these findings; those who look to the young for perennial challenge, inventiveness and change will be saddened by them.

VII

A Bridge to the World

THE SCHOOL AS AGENT

THE SCHOOL can be considered as the agent of parents. On this view it exists to provide services which parents unaided could not provide. The parent is seen as the consumer or client and his wishes carry great weight. Alternatively the school can be considered as the agent of the children, existing to further their interests. The pupil is the client or consumer and, as he gets older, his own view of the services he requires should carry more weight. The school which is the agent of parents does not necessarily provide the same services as the school which is first and foremost the agent of the child—here, the needs, capacities and interests of the child receive an independent, professional assessment which may not coincide with the views of parents.

On the face of it, schools which regard parents as consumers and set out to satisfy their needs are 'democratic': they accept the will of the people. In this sense only our independent schools have a real measure of democracy, and even they may insist on conducting some of their affairs contrary to the wishes of parents. Their main protection in doing so is the requirement of external examinations: they can refuse to fall in with the wishes of parents on the grounds that a variety of examination requirements leaves them no choice. This has been one of the most important functions of external examinations over the past century—to legitimize the school's obstruction of parental demands.

But in general the independent schools offer the services their clients approve—otherwise they would go out of business. The record of the school and its prospectus tell the

consumer what services are offered, and the consumer decides to buy. These services will embrace particular forms
of social, moral and intellectual training.

In America the publicly financed schools approximate to
the independent schools of Britain in their sensitivity to
parents. Teachers are the agents of parents, providing the
services the latter have prescribed. Through their local
organizations parents bring direct pressure to bear on the
schools, even in matters of curriculum and teaching
methods. The Parent–Teacher Associations and local
citizenship committees sponsor candidates for election to the
school boards. The teacher (says George Baron) is seen as
'the instrument of the popular will rather than as the
interpreter of knowledge'.

The teacher is the agent of the family almost to the same
degree as the private, domestic tutor or governess of the
past. She certainly does not have the impudence, any more
than Agnes Grey, to pose as a corrective. She is:

> firmly regarded as the agent of the community which she
> serves. As such she is 'hired'—the word itself is significant—
> not infrequently for a year at a time, and is required to comply
> in not a few cases with rigid conventions governing her off-
> duty life. These may include, in rural areas (although her
> duties are wholly secular), church attendance and Sunday
> school teaching, besides abstinence from alcohol and tobacco.
> Similar, though less passively accepted, constraints are im-
> posed on men teachers. [1]

There is pressure to concede more direct power and influence to parents in English education. Vaizey has put the
parent-as-consumer argument as follows: 'In universities
the teachers have absolute control. In schools, the politicians
and the administrators have the whip hand. Often, the
parents feel that their interests are neglected. They are
represented by neither party.' (This is a curious statement.
As citizens, parents, of course, elect the politicians both
national and local, and presumably approve their educational
policies. As local councillors they presumably not only
approve but determine them.) Vaizey continues: 'It is

important that the primary social unit, the family, should be given due weight. This is a genuine argument for tempering the power of the teaching profession. In this instance the parent is a particular example of the citizen-consumer. His interests are, in general, sovereign, and professional power must be subordinate to them.'[2]

Economists are disposed to a tender regard for consumers. It may be good economics, but it is often bad social philosophy, to regard the consumer as king. There are some things which a democratic community very properly decides are not for sale or subject to the normal pressures of the market place. The English tradition of state education over the past century has been to consider the interests of the child rather than the wishes of the parents. Happily these often coincide; but in case of conflict the tendency has been, where possible, to give weight to the judgement of teachers against that of parents—particularly with regard to curriculum, allocation to particular courses and the minimum age of leaving. Whatever the parent may wish, these matters are not generally under his control.

The broad direction of education is, of course, a matter for national and local electorates; and as voters and councillors parents are not impotent. But within the general framework of public policy teachers have properly acquired something of the professional stature of other professional men. They have the expertness to diagnose their clients' (i.e. the children's) needs to prescribe appropriate educational procedures.

The resolve to secure the same treatment for teachers as for other professional men was clear in the report of the Taunton Commission on endowed grammar schools published in 1868. Whatever their social status, parents were judged (on their record) to be without the knowledge and competence to interfere in the detailed provision of a highly specialized service, as they did with alarming and often disastrous results in the private schools of the day. 'It is quite clear,' the commissioners concluded (Volume 9), 'that it cannot be said, that the majority of parents of the middle classes are really good judges of education . . . of the best means of training the mind, and of strengthening the faculties, they are no judges at all.' Middle-class parents did not place sufficient emphasis on 'the cultivation of the understanding, on the refinement of the thoughts and manners, on what is solid and permanent, rather than on what is showy and transitory . . .'.

Of course teachers have to be up to the job—and it is the business of the teacher training college and university department of education to see that they have the highly specialized skills and knowledge to serve the children effectively. They need the elaborate and sophisticated skills which enable them to assess the capacities, potential and interests of their pupils and to prescribe educational courses and procedures accordingly. It is probable that the power they exercise requires that they become expert educational technologists to a greater degree than they commonly are at present.

It is the inequalities of parents which have made so difficult the pursuit of equal opportunity in English education. As 'consumers' their tastes and demands vary enormously and often bear little relationship to the real needs of the child. The ambitions of parents for their children bear a closer relationship to their social class position than to the demonstrated abilities of their children.

It is the business of education in our social democracy to eliminate the influence of parents on the life-chances of the young. We have abolished nomination to the civil service and the purchase of commissions in the army; with remarkable inconsistency we still allow the purchase of a place at Eton. And some of our allegedly 'progressive' education authorities have introduced nomination by parents of the school their children shall attend.

The alleged abolition of eleven-plus and the substitution of 'parents' choice' is the most retrograde move in the recent history of education. It is tolerable only to the extent that it is bogus, that assessment of abilities is in fact still being made by objective diagnostic tools and children allocated to appropriate courses and institutions on their results. The inequalities of parents are demonstrable: they differ in wealth, in social confidence and competence, in their social range and knowledge and the useful 'contacts' they have made, in their ambitions for their children. Since compulsory schooling in the eighteen-seventies, Mundella's Children's Charter of 1889 and the inauguration of the N.S.P.C.C. in the same year, we have decided that children shall not be at the mercy of their parents. It is the business of a local education authority to see that they are not.

It has been the fashion of late to subject the 'meritocracy' to ridicule. But its most devastating satirists have no alternative to offer. And there is none—except nepotism and the still greater influence of kinship connections and the accident of birth which it has been the whole point of democratic advance over the past century to minimize. The aim and ideal of the meritocracy is purely chance or random association between the status of parents and the eventual, adult status of their children. We are still far from this ideal. The family remains a tremendous influence on the life and prospects of the young. Our educational institutions have the duty to minimize and not to enhance it.

THE SCHOOL AS CORRECTIVE

The school may be seen not so much as the agent as the corrective of parents. We see it in this perspective when we are concerned with the rights and interests of children rather than 'primary social units'.

Many parents realize that they need a corrective or at least a supplement. They may be aware of their own inadequacies and look to the school to provide a remedy for their defects. In a 'difficult' area working-class parents may look to the school to exercise the discipline and control over their children which they can scarcely manage ('they'll take more notice of the teacher than of me'—hopefully). In a well-to-do district of small and rather isolated families, the middle-class parent may look to the school to provide the sociability for his child which the home cannot offer in full measure.

He looks to the school to draw the child out of himself and make him a good mixer. The author has found both these expectations strong in working-class and middle-class parents respectively in surveys in the Midlands.[3]

But families may have deficiencies, from an educational standpoint, which they are unwilling or unable to recognize. They may limit their children's range of social contacts in order to 'protect' them, and may demand that the school reinforce this protection. They may afford little experience of particular skills and areas of knowledge and disapprove of the school paying attention to these skills. Manual workers may feel that their children are being made soft through a bookish education; professional men that the curriculum is over-concerned with 'frills'.

The schools have been inhibited over recent decades in correcting or supplementing the home less by arguments about the democratic rights—or even the consumer rights —of parents than by the apparent certainties of modern sociology. Sociologists have often stressed the need to relate the school and its curriculum to the local environment, to preserve and perpetuate the local 'subculture'; and they are often thought to have shown that home influences are in any case virtually insurmountable. It is this second argument which is perhaps most damaging.

Sociology has become an excuse for educational incompetence. Because the sociologists have demonstrated the handicap of the bad home, this is no reason why the school should not help the child to overcome it—even if this means undermining the sacred and no doubt picturesque subcultural values which it represents. It is still less excuse for steering the able child from such a home away from an academic education on the grounds that he will get little support or encouragement from his parents. And there is small doubt that this happens (and it can probably happen more easily unknown and unchecked when we abandon objective tests of selection in favour of an ill-defined 'guidance'). Mays is very tactful in describing the attitudes of teachers in back-street Liverpool, but observes that special help for borderline candidates for the grammar school was thought unwise 'as this would be at the expense of children coming from "better" homes in the better-off neighbourhoods'.[4]

There are grave dangers in teachers knowing too much about the homes of their pupils, unless their sociological knowledge is more sophisticated than is commonly the case. The child can be damned before he starts. There are still graver dangers if such knowledge enters at all into the prediction of 'good grammar school (or university) material'. Our schools are in the grip of a new and debilitating socio-logical fatalism: predestination based on misunderstood (and generally very low if 'significant') correlation coefficients.

In our social democracy one of the major tasks for educa-tion is quite clear and simple: it is to make the outlook and the prospects of the child from the bad home as good as those of the child from the good home, to provide him with as effective an education. Sociology has not proved that this cannot be done; it has shown that it is more difficult than we once thought, and that schools have got to mobilize themselves for an assault which will counteract the worst of parents.

To achieve this will require from many teachers a more vigorous, imaginative, aggressive and technically competent approach to their work. Even if we think only of academic skills and attainments, there is little doubt that many children from bad homes could do far better if the schools set themselves seriously to the task.

This applies to grammar schools no less than to primary and secondary modern schools. With almost a 40 per cent wastage and failure rate in the nineteen-fifties—in the sense of early leaving or poor O-level examination results—the grammar schools have no grounds for complacency. The Ministry of Education's report on *Early Leaving* gave a 'failure' rate of 38 per cent. These children had either failed to stay the O-level course or had passed in no more than two subjects.

This is, indeed, a shocking and grossly uneconomic performance even by their own criteria of excellence. The early leavers and the low achievers came preponderantly from lower-class homes; but they were children of high intelligence, or they would not have gained a place in the schools in the first place. The grammar schools have failed on a massive scale with children of good intelligence who happen to come from lower-class homes. In the fifties no less than 65 per cent of the grammar school children who came from the homes of unskilled workers were failures in an academic sense (and in the light of evidence on their extra-curricular activities, probably in other senses too). These social class differences are not disappearing. The Robbins Report, *Higher Education* (1963), gives details (Appendix One) of the G.C.E. results of leavers in 1960–1 from the maintained grammar schools. Sixty-three per cent of the children whose fathers were unskilled or semi-skilled manual workers obtained fewer than five O-level passes. But when children came from professional and managerial homes, the grammar schools produced more worthwhile results. Only 28 per cent of these children obtained fewer than five passes at O-level.

The schools are in retreat before bad homes, and on a wide front have capitulated. And many of the homes are not as bad as all that. Many semi-skilled and unskilled workers are ambitious for their children; they even belong to libraries and read books. The back streets of Liverpool's Crown Street district have children of comparable intelligence to other areas of the city, but their eleven-plus examination results are far inferior. The schools are failing to counteract the influence of homes sufficiently for the children to realize their true potential. They are in fact doing much worse than this—in such areas they are failing with able children who are *not* handicapped by home circumstances.

Dr Agnes Crawford, after investigating this situation in Liverpool, was by no means inclined to blame under-achievement squarely on the homes of the area:

> it is clear that some of the parents are interested in their children's education, do use the public libraries, even buy books for the children to read, and for themselves to read.

The proportion of parents who show as much interest as this may be smaller than it is in other parts of the city, but ... their numbers should not be underestimated, nor perhaps their general influence on their neighbours.[5]

The evidence of Douglas's national inquiry is equally clear on this point: bad junior schools are negating the influence of good (i.e. generally supportive) parents. (On the other hand, when schools are good, good parents are superfluous.)

'How far do high standards of teaching in the primary schools make up for lack of interest in the home?' asks Douglas. He recognizes that: 'This is perhaps the most important question in this book.' His data enable him to give a firm answer, and it is worth quoting at length:

> For children at primary schools with a good academic record, the influence of parental interest on performance in the eleven plus examinations is negligible and the same is true of those schools with a poor record. In contrast, children in the rest of the primary schools (i.e. those which sent between 11 per cent and 30 per cent of their leavers to grammar schools) are influenced by the level of their parents' interest.

In the best primary schools the deficiencies of parents are being offset by good teaching, but 'in the worst schools even the children who are encouraged in their work by their parents have no advantage'.

Douglas observes with the restraint, delicacy and tact which characterizes most research workers who have reached the same conclusion: 'By improving the level of teaching in the primary schools it seems that the waste of ability through lack of interest and stimulation at home can be much reduced and perhaps eliminated.' If the schools sustained working-class children in the promise they show at 8 years of age, we should need 50 per cent more grammar school places than are actually available.[6] But they do not. Many—though by no means all—are defeated by the homes they serve.

THE SCHOOL AS A BRIDGE INTO THE WORLD

The task of the schools is formidable. It is not only the influence of the 'bad' home that needs counteracting so that the child can achieve the educational attainment of which he is capable; it is also the influence of the 'good' home, so that the child can make academic progress and still retain his sanity, humanity and zest for living. (What English education needs today above all else—even before the maintenance of largely hypothetical 'standards'—is gaiety, even a touch of *insouciance*. Nothing in life should be as solemn, joyless and pontifical as contemporary higher education and the pronouncements of its arch-priests.)

The second is the more complicated problem. The 'good' school is, perhaps, at present, the one which reinforces the over-demanding and expectant home; the over-driving teacher adds to the pressure of the over-driving father (or mother); and the rather cool and distant personal relationships between parents and child are reproduced in the school (and university) in relationships with teachers. This is admittedly speculative. But there is good evidence in empirical research that grammar school boys much more often than modern school boys see both parents and teachers as negative and hostile towards them.[7]

It is indeed a depressing reflection on mankind if achievement is possible only under such conditions. But it is at least possible that these conditions of home and school are valuable chiefly when we assess achievement, and prepare for its assessment, in particular ways. The formal examination system which we have evolved is perhaps particularly suited to the hard-driven and joyless personality. It gives little reward for spontaneity and creativity, which are admittedly more difficult to assess than the systematic memorizing of information and its deployment to illustrate well-established truths.

Any educational system needs evidence that its aims are being achieved. And today perhaps it is inevitable and even proper that society should expect its educational system to act as a gigantic grading device. (But we need to know much more accurately what our grades really mean in terms of human personality, talent and potential.) We cannot abandon examinations; but we can construct more intelligent examinations. And a holocaust of three-hour written papers is not really very intelligent. While such a method of assessment may be appropriate to some subjects at some stages, it is ludicrous to make it the method for all subjects at all stages from O-level onwards.

In the past the production and display of the 'masterpiece' had perhaps more likelihood of being an exercise of joy; even engagement in the academic 'disputation'. We need to tap new sources of motivation, particularly in our more academic courses. We must seriously apply ourselves to the problem of encouraging and assessing the achievement that comes from joy rather than neurotic drive.

The task of the good school is to find motives for achievement other than—or additional to—the high demands and expectations of authority figures; which express the child's sense of joy rather than his sense of guilt. The good school will not simply be an extension of the 'good' home; on the contrary, it will offer the opportunity for relaxation; the chance to find one's own strengths, interests and enthusiasms.

But if the argument of this book is correct, the 'good' home needs a corrective in other directions too. The school must lead the child out of the claustrophobia of the family in a home-centred society into a wider world of social sympathies, contacts and involvements.

Our schools at the secondary stage must all be comprehensive schools and they must all be public schools. (Of course there must be selection for the particular courses which children follow in the schools.) They must comprehend all social levels and abilities; and they must expose their pupils to a public environment. They must be a bridge into the world, away from the confines of the home whether 'good' or 'bad'. They must offer a planned strategy of exposure to the world.

The School as a Bridge into the World

Schools have progressively limited the intellectual, imaginative and social development of children by restricting the range of human contacts available to them. The result is almost certainly a general impoverishment of development, which has been justified in the past in terms of 'protecting' the young from undesirable influences. But the need for a diversity of contacts representing divergent experiences, opinions and values, for development in moral as well as intellectual directions, is one of the principal conclusions from the life-work of Piaget. We are in danger of sterilizing education to the point of extinguishing all life whatsoever.

Children have been placed in ever more homogeneous groups with regard to intelligence, age and social background (either deliberately in the private schools or as a by-product of segregation by 'intelligence'). Homogeneity with respect to age and ability may perhaps be necessary for actual teaching at some levels and in some subjects. But the adolescent at school should be exposed, under reasonably controlled conditions, to the range of human contacts often available to a seventeenth-century schoolboy attending a public school. In particular the school should not exclude him from all effective contact with adults except his teachers and kinsmen. It was formerly supposed that the child could learn nothing from other children except vice; it is now assumed that he can learn little of value from anybody else. It is one of the oddities of our day that contact between the young and the mature, except certified neuters such as priests, teachers, youth leaders and kinsmen, is regarded as dangerous and even immoral.

Adults other than parents should come into the school—not only as sight-seers on Open Days—to be involved in its affairs: to eat with the children as their guests; to talk with them (but not to lecture them) in small discussion groups; to take part in their drama and their music-making. This might be systematically arranged with a volunteer corps of School Friends. The school must cease to be a fortress heavily guarded against all adults except the staff. Where boarding schools are established—and there must be more of these— the boarding houses should not be on a par with isolation hospitals, but houses in the town, approved lodgings and hostels not exclusively for the use of schoolboys. Some of the less academically inclined adolescents might be still further involved with adults in part-time work. Under such conditions the young will not mark time in an artificially induced immaturity. The fifteen-year-old is not a child, although our present social arrangements are remarkably successful in making him appear like one.

It becomes ever clearer that we have underestimated the potency of the family and overestimated the power of conventional schooling. We have underrated the difficulty of mitigating the restrictive and inhibiting influence which many (not only 'bad') homes can have. If we seriously mean to do justice by all our children and to see them develop to their full stature, it is certain that our thinking and our action with regard to the family as well as the school will need to be more radical, ruthless and courageous.

References

I. THE CHANGING PARENT: THE SUBSTITUTION OF INFLUENCE FOR
POWER

¹ Bernard Bailyn, *Education in the Forming of American Society* (1960).
² Alice Clark, 'How the Rise of Capitalism Affected the Role of the Wife', in J. B. Stern (ed.), *The Family Past and Present* (1938).
³ Ibid.
⁴ Bernard Bailyn, op. cit.
⁵ For a fuller treatment of the thesis advanced in this section see the author's 'Decline of the Educative Family', *Universities Quarterly* (1960), 14.
⁶ Mary Carpenter, *Juvenile Delinquency* (1853). Today the working mother is a frequent scapegoat for our social ills; but American research has failed to establish her as a cause of delinquency: see Sheldon Glueck and Eleanor Glueck, 'Working Mothers and Delinquency', *Mental Hygiene* (1957), 41. For a thorough review of American work on the effect of working mothers on child behaviour and family life in general see F. Ivan Nye and Lois Wladis Hoffman, *The Employed Mother in America* (Chicago, 1963). Both family solidarity and self-confident youngsters appear, in general, to be the outcome of a mother at work.
⁷ K. Friedlander, *The Psycho-analytic Approach to Juvenile Delinquency* (1947).
⁸ J. Bowlby, *Forty-four Juvenile Thieves* (1944).
⁹ David Stow, *The Training System* (1850).
¹⁰ Albert K. Cohen, *Delinquent Boys* (1955).
¹¹ J. B. Mays, *Growing up in the City* (1954).
¹² John Mack, 'Full-time Miscreants, Delinquent Neighbourhoods and Criminal Networks', *British Journal of Sociology* (1954), 15.
¹³ J. and E. Newson, *Infant Care in an Urban Community* (1963).
¹⁴ Bruno Bettelheim and Morris Janowitz, *Social Change and Prejudice* (1964).

II. HOME AND SCHOOL: AN HISTORIC CONFLICT

¹ *Four Periods of Public Education* (1862), p. 132.
² J. Bowlby, *Maternal Care and Child Health* (1951); D. Burlingham and Anna Freud, *Infants without Families* (1944).
³ T. Guthrie, *Seed-time and Harvest of Ragged Schools* (1860).

References

4 B. R. Wilson, 'The Teacher's Role—A Sociological Analysis' *British Journal of Sociology* (1962), 13.

5 P. Sorokin, *The Reconstruction of Humanity* (1948), ch. 10.

6 D. Williams, *Lectures on Education* (1789), vol. ii, p. 291.

7 R. Southey, *The Life of Wesley* (1820), pp. 429–30.

8 S. Kelley (ed.), *The Life of Mrs Sherwood* (1854), pp. 38–9.

9 C. K. Paul, *William Godwin* (1876), vol. I, p. 7.

10 J. H. Harris (ed.), *Robert Raikes* (1899), p. 46.

11 T. Guthrie, op. cit., p. 126.

III. SUCCESS STORY

1 G. Talbot Griffith, *Population Problems in the Age of Malthus* (1926), p. 34.

2 *Registrar General's Statistical Review of England and Wales for the Year 1958* (1960), Part 2, p. 10.

3 J. Hajnal, 'Aspects of Recent Trends in Marriage in England and Wales', *Population Studies* (1947), 1.

4 Paul H. Jacobson, *American Marriage and Divorce* (1959), p. 141.

5 G. Rowntree and N. Carrier, 'Resort to Divorce in England and Wales 1858–1957', *Population Studies* (1958), 11.

6 G. H. Elder, 'Achievement Orientations and Career Patterns of Rural Youth', *Sociology of Education* (1963), 37.

7 F. Musgrove, 'Inter-generation Attitudes', *British Journal of Social and Clinical Psychology* (1963), 2.

8 Peter Marris, 'Social Change and Social Class', *The Listener* (5 November 1959).

9 Talcott Parsons, 'The Social Structure of the Family' in R. N. Anshen, *The Family: Its Function and Destiny* (1959).

10 W. Bell and M. D. Boat, 'Urban Neighbourhoods and Informal Social Relations', *American Journal of Sociology* (1957), 62.

11 See E. Litwak, 'Geographic Mobility and Family Cohesion', *American Sociological Review* (1960), 25.

12 E. Litwak, 'Occupational Mobility and Extended Family Cohesion', *American Sociological Review* (1960), 25.

13 Margaret Mead, 'Social Change and Cultural Surrogates' in C. Kluckhohn and H. A. Murray, *Personality in Nature, Society and Culture* (1948).

14 J. F. Morris, 'The Development of Adolescent Value-judgements', *British Journal of Educational Psychology* (1958), 28.

15 J. Pitts, 'The Family and Peer Groups' in N. W. Bell and E. F. Vogel, *An Introduction to the Family* (1960).

16 M. C. Lucas and J. E. Horrocks, 'An Experimental Approach to the Analysis of Adolescent Needs', *Child Development* (1960), 31.

17 M. W. Riley, J. W. Riley and M. E. Moore, 'Adolescent Values and the Riesman Typology: An Empirical Analysis' in S. M. Lipset and L. Lowenthal, *Culture and Social Character* (1961).

18 R. F. Peck and R. J. Havighurst, *The Psychology of Character Development* (1960).

19 J. F. Morris, *A Study of Value-judgements in Adolescents* (1955), unpub. Ph.D. thesis, London.

20 A. N. Oppenheim, 'Social Status and Clique Formation among Grammar School Boys', *British Journal of Sociology* (1955), 4.

21 M. B. Sussman, 'The Help Pattern in the Middle Class Family', *American Sociological Review* (1953), 18.

22 See B. J. Stern (ed.), *The Family Past and Present* (1938), p. 177.

IV. A THREAT TO SOCIETY

1 *L'Enfant et la Vie Familiale sous l'Ancien Régime* (1960), pp. 456–7.

2 Thomas Guthrie, op. cit., p. 3.

3 Michael Young and Peter Willmott, *Family and Kinship in East London* (1957).

4 J. M. Mogey, *Family and Neighbourhood* (1956).

5 N. Dennis, F. Henriques and C. Slaughter, *Coal Is Our Life* (1956).

6 *Exploring English Character* (1955).

7 Mark Abrams, 'The Home-centred Society', *The Listener* (26 November 1959).

8 A. R. Radcliffe-Brown and Daryll Forde (eds.), *African Systems of Kinship and Marriage* (1950), pp. 43–4.

9 M. Banton, *White and Coloured* (1959), pp. 18, 19, 126.

10 Charlotte Erickson, *British Industrialists: Steel and Hosiery 1850–1950* (1959), p. 47.

11 J. Berent, 'Social Mobility and Marriage' in D. V. Glass (ed.), *Social Mobility in Britain* (1954).

V. THE 'GOOD HOME'

1 J. E. Floud, A. H. Halsey and F. M. Martin, *Social Class and Educational Opportunity* (1956), p. 137.

2 H. T. Himmelweit, 'Social Status and Secondary Education since the 1944 Act: Some Data for London' in D. V. Glass (ed.), *Social Mobility in Britain* (1954).

3 J. W. B. Douglas, *The Home and the School* (1964), p. 170.

4 A. H. Halsey and L. Gardner, 'Selection for Secondary Education and Achievement in Four Grammar Schools', *British Journal of Sociology* (1953), 4.

References

[5] J. P. Lees and A. H. Stewart, 'Family or Sibship Position and Scholastic Ability', *Sociological Review* (1957), 5.

[6] J. P. Lees, 'The Social Mobility of a Group of Eldest-born and Intermediate Adult Males', *British Journal of Psychology* (1952), 43.

[7] *The Psychology of Affiliation* (1959).

[8] E. E. Sampson, 'Birth Order, Need Achievement, and Conformity', *Journal of Abnormal and Social Psychology* (1962), 64.

[9] J. E. Floud *et al.*, op. cit., p. 93.

[10] Ibid., p. 102.

[11] N. Kent and D. R. Davis, 'Discipline in the Home and Intellectual Development', *British Journal of Medical Psychology* (1957), 30.

[12] J. W. Getzels and P. W. Jackson, *Creativity and Intelligence* (1962).

[13] D. R. Brown, 'Personality, College Environment and Academic Productivity.' in Nevitt Sanford (ed.), *The American College* (1962), pp. 536–62.

[14] *Education and the Working Class* (1962), pp. 151–2.

[15] E. Paul Torrance, 'Personality Dynamics of Under-self-evaluation among Intellectually Gifted Freshmen' in E. P. Torrance (ed.), *Talent and Education* (1960).

[16] J. E. Floud *et al.*, op. cit., p. 88.

[17] E. Frazer, *Home Environment and the School* (1959)., p. 66.

[18] G. H. Elder, 'Achievement Orientations of Rural Youth', *Sociology of Education* (1963), 37.

[19] J. and E. Newson, op. cit., p. 217.

[20] Allison Davis, *Social Class Influence upon Learning* (1948).

[21] I. L. Child, 'Socialization' in Gardner Lindzey (ed.), *Handbook of Social Psychology* (1954), vol. 2.

[22] H. J. Hallworth, 'Anxiety in Secondary Modern and Grammar School Children', *British Journal of Educational Psychology* (1961), 31.

[23] R. Lynn and I. E. Gordon, 'Maternal Attitudes to Child Socialization: Some Social and National Differences', *British Journal of Social and Clinical Psychology* (1962), 1.

[24] U. Bronfenbrenner, 'Socialization and Social Class through Time and Space' in E. E. Maccoby, T. M. Newcomb and L. Hartley (eds.), *Readings in Social Psychology* (1958).

[25] J. W. M. Whiting and I. L. Child, *Child Training and Personality* 1953).

[26] F. Musgrove, 'Parents' Expectations of the Junior School', *Sociological Review* (1961), 9.

[27] M. C. Shaw, 'Need Achievement Scales as Predictors of Academic Success', *Journal of Educational Psychology* (1961).

[28] F. L. Strodtbeck, 'Family Interaction, Values and Achievement' in D. C. McClelland *et al.*, *Talent and Society* (1958).

[29] D. C. McClelland *et al.*, *The Achievement Motive* (1953), p. 283.

References

30 G. H. Elder, 'Achievement Orientations and Career Patterns of Rural Youth', loc. cit.

31 D. C. McClelland *et al.*, op. cit., p. 329.

32 W. L. Warner and J. C. Abegglen, *Big Business Leaders in America* (1955). pp. 59 ff.

33 Anne Roe, 'A Psychological Study of Eminent Psychologists and Anthropologists, and a Comparison with Biological and Physical Scientists', *Psychological Monographs* (1953), 67.

34 R. K. Kelsall, 'Self-recruitment in Four Professions' in D. V. Glass, op. cit.

35 C. A. Anderson and M. Schnaper, *School and Society in England* (1952), Tables 2 and 6.

36 Noel Annan, 'The Intellectual Aristocracy' in J. H. Plumb (ed.), *Studies in Social History* (1955).

VI. SATISFACTIONS AT HOME, CLUB, WORK AND SCHOOL

1 R. H. Schaffer, 'Job Satisfaction as Related to Need Satisfaction at Work', *Psychological Monographs* (1953), 67.

2 C. R. Pace and G. G. Stern, 'An Approach to the Measurement of College Environments', *Journal of Educational Psychology* (1958), 49, and G. G. Stern, 'Environments for Learning' in Nevitt Sanford (ed.), *The American College* (1962).

3 Anne McFee, 'The Relationship of Students' Needs to their Perceptions of a College Environment', *Journal of Educational Psychology* (1961), 52.

4 H. C. Lindgren, 'The Use of a Sentence Completion Test in Measuring Attitudinal Change among College Freshmen', *Journal of Social Psychology* (1954), 40.

5 E. Bene, 'The Use of a Projective Technique, illustrated by a study of the differences in Attitudes between Pupils of Grammar Schools and Secondary Modern Schools', *British Journal of Educational Psychology* (1957), 27.

6 P. M. Symonds, 'The Sentence Completion Test as a Projective Technique', *Journal of Abnormal and Social Psychology* (1947), 42.

7 Talcott Parsons, *The Social System* (London, 1964), pp. 48–9.

8 Talcott Parsons and Edward Shils, *Toward a General Theory of Action*, (1951), p. 209.

9 A. Hancock, and J. Wakeford, 'The Young Technicians', *New Society* (14 January 1965).

10 A. Berge, 'Young People in the Orient and Occident', *International Journal of Adult and Youth Education* (1964), 16.

11 C. H. Cooley, *Human Nature and the Social Order* (1922).

12 G. H. Mead, *Mind, Self and Society* (1934).

[13] T. R. Sarbin, 'Role Theory' in G. Lindzey, *Handbook of Social Psychology* (1954), vol. I.

[14] Donald Super, *Career Development: Self Concept Theory* (1963).

[15] James F. T. Bugental and Seymour L. Zelen, 'Investigations into the Self Concept I. The W–A–Y Technique', *Journal of Personality* (1950), 18.

[16] H. M. Kuhn and T. S. McPortland, 'An Empirical Investigation of Self Attitudes', *American Sociological Review* (1954), 19.

[17] *15 to 18* (H.M.S.O. 1960).

[18] William A. Westley and Frederick Elkin, 'The Protective Environment and Adolescent Socialisation', *Social Forces* (1956–7), 35. For other American evidence of the powerful influence of parents on adolescents' values (particularly scholastic aspirations) see J. A. Kahl, 'Education and Occupational Aspirations of "Common Man" Boys', *Harvard Educational Review* (1953), 23.

VII. A BRIDGE TO THE WORLD

[1] G. Baron, 'Social Background to Teaching in the United States', *British Journal of Educational Studies* (1950). Cf. J. W. Getzels and E. G. Guba, 'The Structure of Roles and Role Conflict in the Teaching Situation', *The Journal of Educational Sociology* (1955), 29.

[2] J. Vaizey, *Britain in the Sixties: Education for Tomorrow* (1962).

[3] F. Musgrove, 'Parents' Expectations of the Junior School', loc. cit.

[4] J. B. Mays, *Education and the Urban Child* (1962), p. 151.

[5] Ibid., p. 150.

[6] See D. V. Glass's Introduction to J. W. B. Douglas, *op. cit.*

[7] Eva Bene, 'The Objective Use of a Projective Technique, Illustrated by a Study of the Differences in Attitudes between Pupils of Grammar School and of Secondary Modern Schools', *British Journal of Educational Psychology* (1957), 27.

Select Bibliography

ARIÈS, P., *L'Enfant et la Vie Familiale sous l'Ancien Régime* (Paris: Plon, 1960).

DAVIS, ALLISON, *Social Class Influences on Learning* (Cambridge: Harvard University Press, 1948).

DOUGLAS, J. W. B., *The Home and the School* (London: MacGibbon & Kee, 1964).

FRAZER, E., *Home Environment and the School* (University of London Press, 1959).

GLASS, D. V. (ed.), *Social Mobility in Britain* (London: Routledge, 1954).

MCCLELLAND, D. C. *et al.*, *The Achievement Motive* (New York: Appleton-Century-Crofts, 1953).

MAYS, J. B., *Education and the Urban Child* (Liverpool University Press, 1962).

NEWSON, JOHN and ELIZABETH, *Infant Care in an Urban Community* (London: George Allen and Unwin, 1963).

TOWNSEND, PETER, *Family Life of Old People* (London: Routledge, 1957).

WILLMOTT, P. and YOUNG, M., *Family and Class in a London Suburb* (London: Routledge, 1960).

YOUNG, M. and WILLMOTT, P., *Family and Kinship in East London* (London: Routledge, 1957).

Index

Index